DESTINATION KWAI

'RELUCTANT GYPSY'

By Jack Shuttle

© Jack Shuttle 1994
All rights reserved. No part of this publication may be reproduced or transmitted in any form or by any means without prior permission.

PRINTED & PUBLISHED BY:-
TUCANN*design&print*
19 High Street, Heighington, Lincoln LN4 1RG
Telephone & Fax (01522) 790009

ACKNOWLEDGEMENTS

I express my thanks for the use of the following photographs:-

Air Chief Marshall Sir Nigel Maynard, KCB, CB, CBE, DFC, AFC, and Air Commodore H. A. Probert, MBE, MA on pages 43, 44, 49 and 50.

The Trustees of the Imperial War Museum, London on pages 96, 110, 111, 112, 113, 119, 127, 137 and 182.

The Far East Prisoner of War Association on pages 91, 99, 111, 112, 113, 126, 141, 154

My appreciation is also extended to Mr. S. Gimson, QC of Edinburgh for permission to reproduce his drawings on pages 96, 112, 119 and 137.

CONTENTS

CHAPTER		PAGE
1	KENTISH DAYS AND BEYOND	4
2	FROM SHANGHAI TO SINGAPORE	10
3	MALAYAN INVASION	24
4	SINGAPORE FALLS	35
5	INTO CAPTIVITY	40
6	SELARANG	51
7	DESTINATION KWAI	59
8	WUN LUN	65
9	TARKILEN	82
10	WAMPO SOUTH	89
11	BACK TO CHUNGKAI	95
12	BULGING CHUNGKAI	118
13	1944 AND STILL AT CHUNGKAI	128
14	NAKHON PATHOM	150
15	IT'S ALL OVER	166
16	GOING HOME	174

... I will make you a name and a praise among the people of the earth when I turn back your captivity before your eyes saith the Lord.

CHAPTER 1.

KENTISH DAYS AND BEYOND.

It was a brilliant day, that Sunday 3rd. September, 1939. Dick Coventry and I had just finished our first two-hour stint at 6am and, after resting until 10 o'clock, resumed our guard duties with the sun beating down as it had done since early morning. Within the hour the sirens sounded and we were at war.

This duty heralded the transformation of our lives, for to us twenty-year olds it had seemed like a holiday when on the previous Monday we had received overnight instructions via the police to report the next day to our local Territorial Drill Hall and had then travelled by lorry to Sharnal Street railway station. Despite its name, the station was situated in a rural setting between the villages of Hoo and High Halstow in the county of Kent.

Now things were different. Fate had many varying experiences ahead for the thirty or so of us young soldiers, while I myself was indeed destined for a gypsy kind of life during my service in the 1939/45 War.

For some months we continued to patrol the railway sidings serving the huge Navy underground magazine at Chattenden, our routine unchanged. All the Naval cordite reserves were stored here and at Lodge Hill and we had taken over our duties from regular troops whose guard had been continuously maintained since 1911 when Winston Churchill, then Home Secretary, had discovered to his horror that we were 'naked' at Chattenden. He then hurriedly arranged for the Service Chiefs to dispatch a company of infantry.

The headquarters of A Company, 2/6th Battalion of the East Surrey Regiment, to which we belonged, were located at Chattenden Barracks but our motley crew, billeted at the station, had to sleep fully clothed on the floors of the waiting room and booking office and were constantly on patrol duties of two hours on and four hours off. Ablutions had to be conducted in the public toilets on the platform and we cooked our dry rations in the open goods yard. However, with the approach of winter and the weather turning colder, we made life a little more comfortable by scrounging coal from the obliging passing steam locomotive drivers and their firemen for fueling the waiting room fire.

In November we were relieved and some of our number, including my friend Dick, transferred to the 1/6th Battalion undergoing training at Lyme Regis in Dorset prior to embarking to join the British Expeditionary Force in France. Theirs was to be a distinguished future which was to include Dunkirk, North Africa, Italy and Greece. With them went a young officer, 2nd Lt. Russell, who had recently replaced 2nd Lt. Bradley as our commander at Sharnal Street. Both were to excel in acts of bravery, the former being awarded the Military Cross at St. Valery. The remainder of us moved to battalion headquarters at Richmond in Surrey and were lodged in a house that had formerly been a small private school, parading along the street to the drill hall for meals. At least now we did not have to cook for ourselves and furthermore enjoyed the luxury of sleeping on bed-boards - three planks of wood on small stools, with the outer ones angled for comfort. We were also able to change into night attire for the first time in three months.

It was not to last and after two weeks twenty of us were informed that we were bound for Shanghai in Northern China, to join one of the regular battalions, the 2nd East Surreys who had been stationed there since 1938.

Under the command of 2nd Lt. Barnard and accompanied by six other junior officers, including 2nd Lt. Bradley, we left on Sunday 17th December, 1939, after first having enjoyed seven days embarkation leave. We departed by train from Surbiton to the strains of the song, "We'll meet again, don't know where, don't know when", lustily sung by a group of officers from the 2/6th who had come along to see us off. The train took us into Southampton docks, where we boarded a cross-channel steamer during the afternoon and, after spending the night aboard, disembarked at Cherbourg some twenty-four hours later. Confined to the docks area, we soon found a small cafe and tucked into a meal of steak and eggs; no rations had yet been issued and we had not eaten since breakfasting the previous morning at Kingston Barracks.

By late Monday it was entraining again, this time courtesy of the French Railways. Departing at eleven o'clock we sped on through the night, skirting Paris and on via Verzon over the Blue

Mountains to Marseilles, arriving on Wednesday morning. Here we found awaiting us the Bibby Line SS Nevasa, a 9000 tonnes coal burning troopship of ancient lineage, and we filed aboard in time for a midday meal. There had been no provision whatsoever on the whole journey for meals - that gypsy existence again - and we had fended for ourselves at the stopping stations en-route, so that first lunch was very welcome even though we were to find the fare on our forthcoming six week voyage very average, to say the very least.

We soon settled in to our mess deck and the routine of collecting hammocks from the hold each evening and returning them in the morning. Our group of new seafarers comprised Harry Wise, newly promoted Lance Corporal prior to departure, Jim Bartram and his cousin Arthur, 'Ginger' Butler, Arthur Leatherland, Bob 'Dixie' Deane, 'Tich' Hewitt, Len Rance, Charlie Slade, 'Blondie' Howell, 'Paddy' Truesdale, Don Wells and Fred King from A Company plus three Headquarter Company men - Corporal Ryan and Privates Constable and Edwards. The seven junior officers, 2nd Lts. Barnard, Bradley, Bobe, Colls, Smith, Collins and Bruckmann, were quartered in cabins on a special officers' deck. They had already began to experience the greater comforts afforded commissioned ranks overseas, especially in the Far East.

The ship's complement upon sailing numbered twelve hundred troops, all in drafts of twenty personnel plus varying groups of young officers, our role being to replace experienced soldiers in the regular army serving in Aden, India, Singapore, Hong Kong, and Shanghai. They were to return to the United Kingdom on the same SS Nevasa to assist in the training of the newly conscripted soldiers, the militiamen.

So here we were, travelling abroad for the first time in our lives and into the unknown, in the company of another troopship, the SS Neuralia, which was on a similar mission but bound for Malta and the Middle East. Initially escorted by an armed merchantman which soon dispersed, we made our way to our first port of call, Port Said. Before arrival there we celebrated Xmas and at the impromptu singsong on deck the most popular rendering was, of course, "I'm going to get you on a slow boat to China" a song then, as now fifty-five years later, very much in vogue. Upon mooring we were inundated by the legendary 'bum boat boys' of this infamous port selling their wares which included locally manufactured Gold Flake cigarettes, which was a popular brand sold at home in a very distinctive yellow packet but those on offer here were a very inferior copy. Many were the unworldly soldiers swindled but they were soon to learn the ways of the East.

We regained our land legs by a route march round the town, it being considered that individual leave was not desirable due to the port's unlawful reputation. A day at anchor and we were away again, proceeding along the Suez Canal with much interest to all aboard, into the excruciating heat of the Red Sea and, after a quick call at Aden, on to the Indian Ocean. There followed nearly two weeks of nothing but sea - we never saw a single vessel - and then we were docking at Bombay. We actually were 'East of Suez'. Shore leave was granted on each of the two days here and we soon left the ship dressed in unaccustomed khaki drill uniforms complete with Wolseley helmet type topees. It was just as well we went to shore as there was an immediate invasion by Indian labourers, male and female, re-coaling which produced a film of coal dust that soon settled everywhere.

Now a completely new world greeted us. The sweet and foul smells, the strange 'different' Indians - Hindus and Muslims - thronging the streets which were here and there blocked by their sacred cows; a horse drawn ride in a picturesque gharry to the gate of India, a visit to the Botanical Gardens. It was all so impressionable to young men not so long out of school - geography live! Nowadays it is commonplace to jet anywhere in the world within a few hours but then, well, to us it was just magical.

On next we cruised down to the apex of the Indian Subcontinent to the beautiful island of Ceylon, now of course Sri Lanka. There being no deep sea moorings we alighted by tender and spent another spellbinding day exploring the delights of Colombo.

The following day we moved on again, this time Singapore bound. Our first visit to this fateful place was to be of only two hours duration, just long enough to discharge the Malayan drafts. By now the numbers on board had diminished considerably and this necessitated additional fatigues on the journey through the China Sea, which we shared with our opposite numbers from the Royal Scots and the Middlesex Regiment going to Hong Kong plus the Seaforth Highlanders coming with us to Shanghai. It was not a very pleasant interlude due to the extremely heavy seas, we found controlling food containers whilst working in the galley hard and difficult, so it was with some relief when we duly arrived at Hong

Kong at the end of January, 1940. This was the final destination for the Nevasa so we disembarked and took up temporary residence in the pleasant and comfortable barracks of the 1st Battalion of the Middlesex Regiment at Shumshuipo in Kowloon. The commissioned ranks, traditionally, were even more happily housed at the famous Peninsular Hotel.

The weather in Hong Kong at this time of the year is very similar to a fine warm summer's day in England and we made the most of our short stay here. The regular occupants were away on manoeuvres in the hills of the New Territories so we had the place to ourselves, sharing with the twenty soldiers we were replacing and who had already arrived from Shanghai, homeward bound.

Yet further new experiences greeted us as we visited Hong Kong by crossing from the mainland to the island on the busy Star Ferry. The bustle and background sounds - oh that Chinese music constantly wailing - were so very different from India. We were to become very fond of and grateful to the likeable Chinese in the years to come.

'A' Company 2/6th Batt. East Surreys, Chertsey, August 1939

I bring up the rear as we mount patrol at Sharnal Street station, September 1939.

British India S. N. CO'S.S. "Nevasa" 9,213 tons gross.

CHAPTER 2.

FROM SHANGHAI TO SINGAPORE.

The 2nd Battalion of the East Surrey Regiment, commanded by Lt. Colonel G. E. Swinton, M.C., had been posted to Shanghai at the time of the Munich Crises in 1938. By 1940 they were well established at their neat and tidy barracks in the Great Western Road, with the exception of a company at Jessfield Park some two miles away and another on detachment further north at Tientsen. Despite the onerous duties of policing the large International Settlement, a chore shared with another battalion of the British Army (The Seaforth Highlanders) and American, French and Italian troops, they had maintained their high standards of ceremonial soldiering.

It was into this environment, then, that we arrived on the 5th. day of February, 1940 after having spent an uncomfortable week long voyage aboard a Butterfield & Swire coastal steamer battling through monsoon conditions in the China Sea.

Now, for the first time in over six months service to date, we were given real beds to sleep in, complete with sheets and blankets; there was also an issue of pyjamas to wear. Goodbye gypsy for a while! Our general appearance, having worn the same badly fitting battledress uniforms without change since call-up, presented something of a rabble. Everyone around us was smartly turned out in peacetime service dress and it was quickly decreed that we should be kitted out afresh, so the slovenly battle dress was immediately discarded. The autocratic Col. Swinton had never seen it before and was absolutely appalled.

The first priority was to turn us into proper soldiers. Having only joined the Territorial Army just before the outbreak of the war we had received very little training and now here we were, expected to be as proficient as our compatriots in this crack regiment. The senior Warrant Officer, Regimental Sergeant Major Ted Worsfold, M.B.E. decided to take us in hand personally and he must surely have considered it as something of a challenge. There followed three weeks of concentrated arms drill from dawn to dusk in the bitterly cold Siberian like weather of Northern China. Miraculously at the end of the period we really had become soldiers and eligible for posting to our various companies for regular duties. It felt **good**. Some, including Charlie Slade and Len Rance joined 'B' Company with me and the remainder were evenly distributed throughout the battalion. The R.S.M. had done his job well!

Life from now on consisted of guard mounting conducted with much pomp and ceremony, street patrols and periodic five day stints manning the outposts on the boundaries separating the International Settlement and Japanese controlled Greater Shanghai. Between times we fitted in weapon training - I became quite adept, to my surprise, at stripping and reassembling a Bren machine gun in times calculated in seconds - and there were also visits to the firing range, where I was not so expert by any means.

Eventually our backgrounds were investigated and those with clerical experience selected for office employment; Harry Wise, Blondie Howell and I joined the staff in the Orderly Room, which was the administration nerve centre of the battalion. Harry was to remain a part of that organization, becoming a key functionary and subsequently being promoted to the rank of Lance Sergeant. Shortly after starting these duties there arose a requirement for a company clerk with Headquarter Company and, although I had only perfunctory knowledge of the necessary typing requirement, I applied for the post and was selected.

I moved from the barrack room into an individual one adjacent to the office, living over the shop as it were, and immediately started concentrated typing practice. A company clerk is something unique for a private soldier, being the confidant of both the company commander and sergeant major and privy to secret information sometimes even denied the senior noncommissioned officers. I soon settled into my new surroundings and seemed to give satisfaction to Captain Andrews and his C.S.M., 'Chinky' Marshall.

By April the weather had changed and we adopted smart khaki drill shirts and shorts worn with hosetops and ankle puttees, the severe winter having given way to tropical conditions. The next month brought saddening news from Europe and the evacuation of the British Expeditionary Force at Dunkirk prompted me to write home:-

OUR CAUSE

In our dear country, so far away
has come, unbelievably, this sunny day,
dangers, hardships and a struggle true
caused by man's war which deep down all must rue.

But our cause is just and so we must fight
to defend our dear islands with all our might:
Whilst here in one of the corners of our Empire
I'm thinking of you back there doing the job without tire.

Though at various times all hope seems to have gone
you will come through, on top, singing a song.
For some it will call for the supreme sacrifice
but there's more in all this than just 'throwing a dice'.

Because justice is justice
and right is right
we will tolerate nothing else before man's sight:
So carry on, dear countrymen, with all your might.

***

Jingoistic? Well, yes, perhaps it seems so nowadays, some fifty years on, but they were traumatic, dangerous days and that was how we all felt. My friends left behind at Richmond the previous December, reinforced by drafts of new conscripts, had departed for France in the April - ostensibly for field training. Soon they were involved in fierce fighting in the defence of St. Valery en Caux, thereby contributing greatly to the success of the Dunkirk evacuation. There was no relief for them and the reward, for most of the survivors, was five long years in German captivity.

Shanghai, 1940. Seething, teeming, pulsating, wicked! Affluence rubbed shoulders with extreme poverty. From the Bund facing the Whangpoo River, along Nanking Road to the junctions with Yu-Yuen and Bubbling Wells Roads, pass the racecourse and into the French Concession the millions thronged in great confusion to the blare of the traffic, intermingled with cries of the rickshaw coolies and others trotting along bearing their incredibly heavy loads. At night the neon lights shone with dazzling brightness as the flood of humanity continued unabated. Plush hotels and smart restaurants abounded together with numerous departmental stores, the Wing On matching any emporium in Europe or the United States. Night clubs and bars proliferated, one street in particular which stretched from Avenue Joffre to Avenue Edward VII comprising such establishments entirely was dubbed 'Cabaret Street' or 'Blood Alley', so called due to its reputation for fights between visiting sailors and soldiers from the local garrisons. Many of the dance hostesses were White Russians who, because of the predominantly aristocratic background of the large refugee community, invariably claimed to be princesses.

Our barracks were a few miles from the Bund on the western outskirts of the International Settlement and faced directly on to the Western Road. In a somewhat paradoxical situation we were surrounded by attractive English middle class houses in neat pleasant avenues, much like the stockbroker belt in Surrey, and the shanty town slums of the poor Chinese refugees from the 1937 battles of the Sino-Japanese War during which the nearby suburb of Chapei had been razed to the ground. Its vast wastes could be quite clearly seen from the perimeter posts on the boundary defined by the Hangchow-Shanghai Railway. The area, universally known as the 'Badlands', was the home of gangsters whose activities rivalled those in Chicago; murder, kidnapping and robbery were rife. In addition Wang Chin Wei, the former Chiang Kai Chek deputy who had become the Japanese puppet leader of an alternative Chinese government in Nanking, maintained a residence in the locality and his police force, the Tao To, were very troublesome. They continuously encroached into the areas that were under the jurisdiction, by treaty, of the Shanghai Municipality Police.

All these factors, with the Japanese acting provocatively at all times, made our duties of keeping law and order very heavy and it required much skilful diplomacy by our commanding officers to avoid the occurrence of ever threatening incidents.

To exacerbate the situation there was the problem of the French and Italian troops. When Italy entered the war on the side of Germany and then the local French Commandant opted to be loyal to the Vichy Government, special measures became necessary to keep us apart. The French Concession was placed out of bounds and we were restricted to certain areas of the International Settlement only. To enforce this, patrols of six military policemen, two each of British, Italian and American, covered the streets demarcating the territory allocated. A special problem arose in April when the film 'Gone With The Wind' arrived and was showing at the popular Roxy cinema which, unfortunately for us, was in the Italian area. To ensure that we did not miss this epic, arrangements were made with the cinema management for a private performance to be given one morning at the Grand in Bubbling Well Road, to which the whole battalion were taken in a convoy of buses.

Another abnormality was the presence of a large German population, a mixture of Nazi sympathizers and Jewish immigrants. The Nazis openly flew the swastika over the German club and operated propaganda radio stations, even featuring a local version of 'Lord Haw-Haw'. To counter these activities there was a British broadcasting station operated in true BBC. style, but mostly listened to was the American-run 'Station X.M.C.A.' which was presented by the fast-talking, likeable Carroll Alcot. This was my introduction to commercial radio and his programmes featured different sponsors daily; when Carroll read his accurate, pro-British news bulletins, he always began with the greeting, "Hello, hello, hello", before going on to plug the advertisement of the day. Thus when it was the turn of the American custard powder manufacturer Jello we heard instead "Jello, jello, jello". Other catch phrases were, *"Have you drunk your Maxwell House coffee?"*, or *"Get your Hermes baby typewriter"* and *"Don't forget to spray your Flit, have you got your flit gun yet?"* Radio X.M.C.A. also played requests and listening was a must, especially as some practical joker in our midst would often send the occasional love message to his sergeant major!

It was not long before I had acquired a very smart set of 'blues', being a dark blue gabardine uniform with red piping extending down out the outside of the trouser legs. It also came with an elegant blue peaked cap. This was the East Surrey walking-out dress which derived from their association with the marines back in the eighteenth century.

How soon we had become soldiers!

When off duty we were permitted to be out of barracks from 4pm until 12.20am and so attired, in the company of Len Rance, I set off on 29th June, 1940 by bus and then rickshaw into town to celebrate my twenty-first birthday. But before hand it was necessary to pass muster before the guard commander, after whose inspection we received clearance to leave the precincts but not before being issued with a box containing the obligatory condoms. This measure was one of the precautions that had to be introduced to stop the spread of the venereal disease that was so prevalent there. In another effort to contain the scourge a number of prophylactic ablution centres, manned by Royal Army Medical Corps personnel, were located in the most popular parts of the city and anyone consorting with the local women was under strict instructions to make use of the facilities immediately it was possible to do so. People becoming infected who had not been recorded as attending would be considered by the military authorities as having incurred self-inflicted wounds making them unfit for duty. This entailed severe punishment, including the withdrawal of all privileges plus a penalty reducing their pay for periods up to a year.

Arriving at the Union Jack club for tea, Len and I next enjoyed seeing a film at the magnificent Grand cinema after which it was back to the club to tuck in to a four course meal. Returning all the way back by rickshaw I still had a little change left from the $5 we had taken out with us, the cost of living being so low that the little jaunt entailed an expenditure less than the equivalent of a two shillings *(10p)*. Upon re-entering the barracks there was a reversal of the ritual at the guardroom, once again we had to be inspected by the guard commander before being allowed in.

We duly handed back the said condoms.

In a letter to my fiancee the next day I was to include the following extract:-

30th June 1940

"Darling Joan,

I was 21 yesterday so I am a man at last. I celebrated it very quietly, with five Shanghai Dollars *(one $ = 4 1/2d. at today's rate)*. However I went out for the first time in six weeks. This is how I spent the money with such munificence. To start with, a bus ride and then rickshaw into town for tea followed by a shave and a haircut. After this on to the cinema to see Edward G. Robinson in Dr. Erlich's Magic Bullet. Thence on to the Union Jack club for a four course meal.

Not the 21st I had planned, darling. And so:-

TONIGHT, MY DARLING JOAN, I WISH THAT WE COULD BE TOGETHER ONCE AGAIN AT HOME DEAR SWEET OLD HOME, LAUGHING, PLAYING, LOVING DEAR IN THE THROES OF REVELRY; BUT ONE DAY, SWEETHEART, I'LL BE BACK, NEVER MORE TO ROAM.

Yours with love, forever,
Jack."

Eventually London decided that the two British units would be more useful elsewhere and towards the end of August we prepared to leave. In their stay of nearly two years the battalion had become very popular with the local inhabitants, Chinese and European alike. The football team had competed successfully in the Shanghai league and the excellent band under their conductor, Bandmaster Manley, were always in great demand. Just before departure the band staged a concert in aid of the 'Buy a plane for Britain' fund and raised a substantial sum to add to the 48000 Shanghai dollars (£800) realized by a battalion collection. We were mightily proud of this effort which was equivalent to fifteen shillings each (75p), especially bearing in mind that our pay was only ten shillings (50p) nett per week, although of course the higher ranks and some of the longer serving other ranks received slightly more.

It was therefore with considerable emotion that we paraded on the 24th of August, 1940 and proudly made our farewell march through the Settlement with the United States Marines band paying us the honour of 'trooping' us over the Garden Bridge boundary to the strains of *"Will ye ne're come back again"*. Crossing the bridge we entered the Japanese occupied territory of Hongkew where the docks were located and, boarding a Jardine & Mathieson steamer, the Wing San, were soon sailing away down the muddy yellow waters of the Whangpo river.

Destination unknown, despite much conjecture, we bypassed Hong Kong and after ten days or so of fairly rough seas serenely steamed through the Singapore Roads surrounded by lush green islands. Our journey's end. This was my second arrival at the delightful port, having moored there on our outward travels the previous January when we stayed only for a few hours to disembark drafts Singapore bound. We did not go ashore then but now we were soon leaving the vessel and being transported to Changi, about fourteen miles on the far north east of the island. Accommodation turned out to be under canvas - obviously the spirit of that gypsy must have left board of the Nevasa here and was awaiting me!

After the brashness of Shanghai I was entranced with the relaxed aromatic beauty of Malaya as we travelled along the East Coast Road, passing Kallang aerodrome and on through Geylon and Betong villages. Coconut and rubber trees were in abundance, the only jarring note in the scenery being the forbidding Changi jail to which at that time we paid scant attention. Our tented camp was established on the Padang, an open area normally used for sporting activities, which was situated adjoining the main Changi Road a mile or so from the pretty Changi village close to the sea. Unbelievably it is now a part of Singapore International Airport! On the other side of the road from us stood Roberts Barracks, the home of the 11th Coast Regiment of the Royal Artillery.

Construction of the Changi cantonment commenced in 1927, having been reclaimed from jungle and swamp. The developers were indeed farsighted and much more than a military camp evolved; it was in fact almost like a garden city with the many beautiful shrubs, together with many natural stately trees preserved by the planners, creating an area of great beauty. The barrack blocks, two-storey flat roofed buildings with open verandas, constructed in concrete and resplendently painted white, glittering in the brilliant sunshine presented a most attractive appearance.

Beyond Roberts Barracks, which consisted of some half dozen blocks, stood Kitchener Barracks occupied by the Royal Engineers which was yet another complex in the same mould. The whole area was connected by a network of undulating roads, all tarmacadamed and neatly grass verged. There were simply magnificent officers messes at both Fairy Point and Temple Hill, handsome bungalows for married quarters, separate messes for sergeants and corporals, N.A.F.F.I. canteens, a Royal Engineers Institute, a garrison school, cinema and guard rooms all built in the same style in dazzlingly white concrete.

Due to the distance from Singapore town numerous squash and tennis courts were also provided and in addition fine padangs provided excellent hockey, cricket and football pitches. Although adjacent to the sea swimming was restricted, by the prevalence of sharks, to the Fairy Point pagar but a fresh water pool existed about two miles down the Changi Road at Selarang. This was yet another barracks of seven similar blocks where a battalion of the Gordon Highlanders were in residence.

It was into this environment then that we arrived. Albeit housed in makeshift tents, after the vicissitudes of Northern China it was sheer bliss even though we were tinged with some envy of the gunners and engineers in their more comfortable surroundings. By now Captain Andrews had assumed command of 'B' Company and soon I returned as well, again as company clerk to work with a new sergeant major, Bob Weston, who was a fine popular veteran soldier. His pride and joy was an old fashioned moustache with waxed ends until one day when we had moved into Northern Malaya some wag snipped them off during his afternoon nap! He was not pleased.

The battalion quickly readjusted to its changed role but after two months we bade farewell to Changi - we were to return later in unfortunate circumstances - and moved to a hutted camp that had been specially erected for us in the grounds of the Chinese High School at Bukit Timah Road, two miles from the centre of Singapore City. Policing duties behind us, training began in earnest in the form of field exercises over Bukit Timah Hill, Buena Vista Gap and Reformatory Road. Ceremony was not forgotten, however, and the regular Commanding Officer's Parade, formerly carried out with much panache on the main square at our Shanghai Barracks, was now conducted on the concourse of Bukit Timah Racecourse.

Being near the centre of Singapore life was not unpleasant. The British residents were generous in their entertainment, organizing a number of concerts and at Christmas inviting us to a ball specially held at the Memorial Hall. Sporting activities had resumed, our football, hockey and rugby teams proving an equal match to those of the local garrison which included Scottish units of the Argyll & Sutherland Highlanders and the Gordon Highlanders plus two English Battalions of the Manchester and Loyal Regiments.

But it was not to last.

In February, 1941 the 'gypsy' struck again and yet once more I was on the move, when we departed by train from Singapore station bound for Alor Star in Kedah State at the far north of the peninsula, 600 miles away and adjacent to the Thailand border. After a hot and sticky two day journey we detrained and then marched along the metal road until reaching the tenth milestone before turning off into the shadows of a rubber plantation. Here had been built our latest home, a camp of wooden huts roofed by atap - our very first introduction to these fronds of the palm tree. The trees were still being tapped for their latex daily by rubber planters and they were not too happy about our presence.

The new camp was called Tanjong Pau, soon to be referred to by all as TJP. There was no electricity, lighting being provided by kerosene lamps and we were located on the edge of thick jungle, just nineteen miles from the Thai border, near the village of Jitra. No sunshine penetrated the area due to the roof of closely planted rubber trees and obviously life was going to be tough. For some it was to be their last home!

In tropical uniform Shanghai, June 1940

"How soon we had become soldiers".

With Charlie Slade in 'B' Co. barrack room.

I man 'W' Post with Len Penfold, right, in Great Western Road, Shanghai. April 1940.

Nanking Road, Shanghai viewed from the Race Course.

The Bund, Shanghai.

A rickshaw awaiting hire outside Great Western Road Barracks.

Bubbling Well Road at night showing the Grand Cinema on the left.

Chinese coolies carrying their heavy loads.

Great Western Road barracks March 1940. A fire breaks out at adjoining premises.

The fire brigade arrives.

Quartermaster Capt. Gingell & Provost Sergeant Wildman direct operations.

A fire picket goes to the assistance of the fire brigade.

We protect 'B' Company lines with corrugated iron sheeting.

23

CHAPTER 3.

MALAYAN INVASION.

The battalion had joined the 11th Indian Division which was of only two brigades instead of the normal complement of three, a factor that was to be of consequence subsequently. The 6th Brigade was commanded by the tall, impressive Brigadier Lay and comprised ourselves together with the 1/8th and the 2/16th battalions of the Punjab Regiment. The other brigade, the 15th, were located at Sungei Patani in Southern Kedah in whose ranks were another British unit, the 1st Leicestershire, plus two more Indian battalions.

The so proud days of regimental soldiering were now over and rigorous battle training was the priority; with the recent occupation by the Japanese of French Indo China the threat and their intentions had become obvious. Nevertheless, Colonel Swinton maintained his rigid disciplinary regime, for instance falling leaves from the umbrella of the rubber trees were not to be tolerated on the ground and these had to be collected and disposed of as they fell. These orders prompted Private Blackman to draw a cartoon depicting a soldier darting out from behind a tree, reaching with an outstretched hand to catch a leaf in midair, which he pinned to the door of the commanding officer's office. As his work was well known from contributions published in the regimental magazine back in Shanghai days, he was soon apprehended and received seven days detention in the guard room for his 'insolence'.

It was, though, important to keep morale at its highest possible level, difficult when we were virtually locked into the camp area, as there was nowhere to go in our free time except for walks in the surrounding dense jungle. The town of Alor Star, about twelve miles distant, was in no way westernized and presented few facilities for outings. Neither were there any public transport services. To help in this regard a mobile cinema was installed, using a generating set that was rather unreliable, which was soon operating in a converted barrack room to provide some welcome entertainment. The floor of this hut had been removed and replaced by poles on which we sat with our feet on the bare ground, the projector being positioned on a platform at the rear. The arrangement worked reasonably well although there was much barracking when latecomers' shadows were cast on the screen as they took their places. For other diversions, on most evenings, the admirable Corporal 'Dolly' Gray conducted Tombola *(bingo)* sessions in the canteen whilst the excellent band still managed to find time to play outside the Officers Mess on the weekly Regimental Nights.

The dank camp conditions in the extremely humid atmosphere, combined with day and night exercises of several days duration in the thick jungle, often conducted in the heavy rainstorms prevalent in the area, led to the organization of change of air breaks. Eighty miles to the south off the west coast stood the island of Penang and it was here that the Sandilands rest camp was established, under the management of C.S.M. Shemmings. By Easter relays of parties began to be sent to the pleasant hutted camp adjacent to the beach for a seven day holiday and it is difficult to convey the sheer joy we all felt, when our turn came around, to be coming out into the world once more.

At about this time a draft arrived from the United Kingdom and I was surprised and pleased that among them were three friends from my home in Egham, Surrey. They were Len Marshall, Bert 'Gunner' Irwin and Charles 'Ches' Chessman and the last time I had seen Len was on my seven days of embarkation leave in December, 1939. I was travelling home from Richmond and he had joined my train at Twickenham where he was serving in the War Reserve Constabulary and, being six years my senior, was confidant of not having to go into the forces. Seeing me in uniform and upon learning that I was bound for the Far East he chortled and when we parted he bade me farewell until after the War had ended. Now here he was ..! The age group exemptions had been lowered in 1940, he was duly conscripted into the East Surreys and when they reached Tanjong Pau I could not resist appearing from behind a rubber tree with the greeting, in Stanley/Livingstone fashion, *"Private Marshall, I presume?"*

'Ches', a butcher by trade, was soon employed in that capacity in the cookhouse - the regular army that we had become part of made skilful use of the civilians entering their midst.

The reunion with 'Gunner' Irwin was unhappily a sad occasion. A recent letter from home had informed me that, whilst his troopship was in the process of sailing from Greenock on the Clyde in January, a German bomb had destroyed his home, killing his wife and seriously maiming their infant child. I had reported the facts, of which he was still unaware, and upon confirmation Padre Babb took him to a quiet part of the jungle at Chunlun to break the news. He accepted the situation with great stoicism and was sent with me on the welcome week's break at the Penang Rest Camp where I was able to offer, by my familiar company, some measure of comfort.

During June a notice appeared in Divisional HQ orders detailing a requirement for a pay and messing accountant at Penang Fortress. At this time my job was still company clerk and Captain Hill, who had superseded Captain Andrews, recommended me for the post. I was selected and, with Len taking over my duties in the company office, I packed my kit and departed for pastures new, never again to return to the Surreys. It was difficult to believe my luck, not at leaving my many friends, but to being posted away to beautiful Penang - it was to bring such a change in my living conditions.

A few miles to the north west of Georgetown, the capital and only town on the island, opposite a small seaplane base at Batu Uban and near to the famous Snake Temple, stood Glugor Cantonment. Built on high ground and approached by a winding road from below, here was a miniature version of the Changi development comprising similar imposing white concrete buildings. What a contrast to Tanjong Pau - that 'gypsy' was being kind again!

My arrival coincided with the formation of Area Details, a new unit administering the hundred or so garrison troops from the Royal Artillery, Royal Engineers, Royal Signals, Royal Army Medical Corps and others like myself on posting. Captain Lindsay-Vears was the Garrison Adjutant and Battery Quartermaster Sergeant 'Mickey' Heald, Private Gilbey from the Royal Army Service Corps and I - now a Corporal - completed the team. Lindsay-Vears was a man of advancing years who had served as a major in the First World War and was a local resident who had volunteered specifically to release a younger officer from having to fulfil these duties. He was one of life's rich characters. Of substantial means, he was a prominent figure on the Malayan racing circuit as the owner of a string of racehorses and was also a big game hunter of some repute. He dealt in the supply of wild animals, particularly tigers, to zoos throughout the world and was a friend of the Rajah of Kedah, who was later to become the first Prime Minister of the newly independent Malaysia - the famous Tunku Abdul Rahman. Lindsay had furthermore at one time been aide-de-camp to the Sultan of Perak but now he was one of us and would arrive at the office each morning chauffeured by his Malay syce in a large black Buick limousine with gleaming white tyres, smoking the inevitable cigar in an ivory holder. A biggish brown leather bangle would adorn his wrist and the mornings were occupied by either Mickey or myself inducting him into the perplexities of army paperwork and accountancy procedures. I am not sure if these were ever mastered and he relied on us implicitly to ensure that he always signed the many documents in the right places. Some weekends he was away racing and whenever one of his horses won he would bring us presents, saying that they were the result of bets placed on our behalf. He was like a breath of fresh air.

There now ensued a pleasant few months for me. Most Sundays were spent on one of the island's lovely beaches, golden sands ringed by coconut and palm trees; the Sandilands Hotel provided excellent curry tiffins which we enjoyed on a terrace by the water's edge. My constant companion was Tony Clifton-Griffiths , also on posting from The East Surreys, and together we explored the locality. One such outing was a motor trip around the island, a distance of about 45 miles. Hiring a taxi, after the customary bargaining, we set off on tour in leisurely fashion along the coast road north, stopping at the Penang Swimming Club for lunch beside the pool. Our journey then took us through the delightful rural countryside, passing rubber plantations in the high central hills and areas of padi fields down in the vales. Further on we saw groves of banana, betel nut and tapioca mingling with fields of pineapples growing in abundance. It was all so refreshing after the rigours of TJP.

There were other excursions. Once we took a bus ride to the village of Ayer Itam to visit Penang Hill, ascending its 2600 feet by means of the near perpendicular cable car. From the summit we had a marvellous view of the whole island, as well as the magnificent Kedah Peak away in the distance. On another occasion we took in the Snake Temple which, being just down the road, was a must. It contained many venomous vipers, a local variety known as gajah kapak *(elephant viper)*, which were coiled everywhere around the joss stick stands and the altars of the Taoist shrine. No doubt their lassitude had something to do with the constantly burning incense, but we kept clear just in case. At night there were numerous quality cinemas showing the latest films and at the Elysee Cabaret Club we danced with the taxi-girls at four dances per dollar.

But the war clouds were gathering. Our prominent white buildings had by now been painted black and air raid precautions practised more earnestly. As we awoke on Sunday 8th December, 1941 it was raining heavily and Signalman Nash, a despatch rider, arrived back from a night mission to divisional headquarters at Sungei Patani with information that the Japanese had attacked across the Thai border and had also landed at Khota Baru. A day of gloom.

Penang Fortress was a misnomer. Apart from our small group of Area Details, the garrison commanded by Brigadier Lyon comprised just one battalion of Punjabis, another of the Local Defence Volunteers *(rubber planters and businessmen)* and two batteries of the 11th. Coast Regiment of the Hong Kong and Singapore Royal Artillery. The latter were there to man searchlights and also the six inch calibre guns of the fixed defences, but not all of their equipment had yet arrived - Malaya was a low priority in London for supplies. Anti-aircraft defences did not exist. The Punjabis left immediately to join up with the 11th Division on the mainland and the Volunteers followed them shortly afterwards.

Scant air cover was provided by just five Brewster Buffalo fighters based on the Butterworth aerodrome on the mainland at Prai.

At 9.30 am precisely on Tuesday 10th December Japanese aircraft, in perfect formation, appeared in the sky above us in groups of twenty-seven. They were attacked by the valiant Brewsters but by the end of the raid all five were gone, one being shot down immediately above our heads; as the pilot, Battle of Britain veteran Flight Lt. Vigars, bailed out he was encircled and machine gunned all the way down to the ground. Fortunately, though, he survived unscathed. A total of some seventy bombers made a concentrated attack that day on Georgetown, their bombs falling on the crowded streets in broad daylight, causing thousands of casualties among the poor unsuspecting inhabitants. The only response we could offer was small arms fire, which was completely useless but at least gave us some encouragement personally. There was a mass exodus of the local civilians that evening, hordes taking to the hills, turning the place into a ghost town overnight. The atmosphere was weird.

The next morning we helped the Civil Administration with the gruesome task of removing the putrefying dead for burial and whilst doing so experienced further raids. These continued at exactly 10.30 am daily, using a lesser number of twenty-seven planes in waves of nine.

Events on the mainland soon decreed that Penang was untenable and we received orders to prepare for evacuation. We immediately commenced denial destruction of all our equipment and vehicles, so my brand new typewriter, accepted with much pleasure only a few months before, had to go. I damaged it with vigorous blows with my rifle and then hurled it down on to the concrete ground below. Leaving Glugor Cantonment on Tuesday 17th December to board a vessel bound for Singapore, we fully expected the daily air raid and spent several hours busily loading it with much trepidation. The gods were with us, though, and for the first time the attackers were absent. We really were a sitting target, being completely exposed. In the meantime, over in Kedah, my poor gallant Surreys were being decimated.

Soon after my departure from Tanjong Pau in July, training had been interrupted by the need to construct fixed defences but, before these could be completed, it was decided by Malaya Command that the best means of defence would be the occupation of Southern Thailand to prevent any proposed Japanese landing at Singora. This entailed a completely new training programme as a mechanized force, at which the battalion quickly became adept. For a whole week before the fateful 8th December they had been ready, actually sitting in their vehicles, awaiting the order to advance. This was never received due to the War Office in London delaying instructions IN FEAR OF VIOLATING THAI NEUTRALITY. The Japs dispensed with such niceties.

Upon the enemy landing dispersal orders were given and they belatedly reverted to manning the old unfinished positions. Here they were immediately engaged in the Battle of Jitra and many, including my friend Ernie Berkeley, fell in that familiar jungle village and the confines of the nearby Tanjong Pau - that unhappy place.

With no air cover they were soon driven back through Alor Star and, with the survivors of the remainder of the division who had also sustained large casualties, occupied new positions at Gurun. It was at Jitra where Colonel Swinton broke a leg in a motor cycle accident when touring his battalion's positions and was replaced by Major Dowling, his second-in-command. A strong enemy force rapidly launched an attack, making full use of tanks *(we had none because the High Command had advised such equipment would be useless in jungle conditions)* giving the division another severe mauling. It was so bad that units from 3rd Corps had to relieve them to enable regrouping.

So many were lost here. On the night of the 14th a conference was called by Brigadier Lay, during which the Brigade Headquarters was attacked and all of the officers attending, with the one exception of the Brigadier, were killed.

They included some of the company commanders, among them Capt. Kerrich of the East Surrey's 'D' Company. In the field ambulance post attached to the HQ a considerable number of wounded were being attended to by the medical officer and Padre. None were spared, all being unceremoniously slaughtered. One of the unfortunates was Jim Bartram, from our intrepid twenty who had ventured forth on the Nevasa two years earlier.

Major Dowling's new command ended when he was caught in the machine gun crossfire - Tom Kinsella, his batman, told me later that the force of the bullets had 'spun the Major round like a top'. Capt. Bradley, our first commander in the early days of Sharnal Street when he was a newly fledged 2nd Lt., perished firing a Bren gun from his hip in the main street of Gurun village and two other members of our Nevasa contingent to die here were Lieutenant Smith and Private 'Tich' Hewitt. Capt. Hill, my former company commander who had recommended me for my posting to Penang, was cut off and succumbed to exhaustion in the jungle.

So heavy were the casualties that the two brigades, now reduced to half strength, had to amalgamate - The East Surreys and Leicestershires uniquely joining forces as the British Battalion under the command of Lt. Col. Morrison.

The 11th Division commander, Major-General Murray-Lyon, despite the lack of supplies and indecision of the government in London, bore the brunt of the reversal. He was promptly relieved and despatched to India, to be replaced by Brigadier Paris from the 12th Brigade who had been in Malaya since 1939. Withdrawal had now reached the Ipoh area and the next battle involving the British Battalion was at Kampar, where on New Year's day the Japanese attacked in strength. Although the battalion had by now many cases of malaria to cope with it held out firmly. However, due to the usual lack of air cover and the continued absence of any naval support, it was relatively easy for the enemy to 'leapfrog' by sea and encircle the defending forces from behind. So yet another retreat was ordered.

Len Marshall, when I met up with him again, commented, "We mowed them down in droves, Jack, and could have stayed put forever."

Lt. General Percival, General Commanding Officer, was to record later that "At the Battle of Kampar our troops fought extremely well, proving that the trained British troops were at least the equal of the best Japanese". Some of the Surreys were to receive awards afterwards for conspicuous bravery. Capt. Vickers, who had succeeded in command of 'B' Company, won the Military Cross and his immediate companions in a gallant counter attack, Sergeant Craggs and Private Graves, the Distinguished Conduct Medal and Military Medal respectively. Kampar now graces the Regimental Battle Honours.

I lost two more of my friends in this encounter. My 21st birthday companion Len Rance was hit by a mortar bomb as he was descending from his truck, whilst Micky Long died bravely trying to knock out a machine gun post single-handed. Bob Deane, from our original draft, received gun shot wounds in his groin but happily survived.

Withdrawal now followed withdrawal, usually by night with forced marches of up to forty miles. By the 19th January they were some 500 miles south of Jitra in the area of Batu Pahat, in terrain consisting of heavy jungle and mangrove swamps leading to the coast about seven miles away. Yet once again a large enemy force had landed behind, but the town was held for one week whilst the defenders waited to be relieved. Desperate attempts to do so were made by the inexperienced 53rd Brigade, an advance group from the newly arrived 18th Division, but to no avail. Orders were received to make their own way to the coast where the navy, in a rare presence, took the survivors off in sloops and landed them in Singapore. Brigadier Challen, who had superseded Brig. Lay in command, was among the many not to rendezvous. The beleaguered and exhausted brigade were once again re-grouped and took their place in the final defence of Singapore Island.

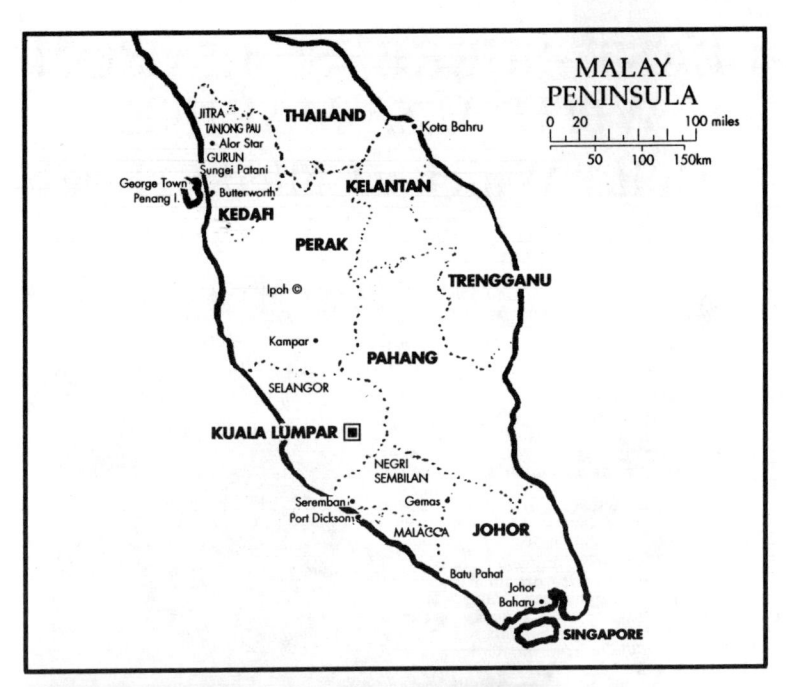

At Tanjong Pau, Jitra some 12 miles north of Alor Star, Kedah.

Relaxing on the beach at Sandilands, Penang Island, August 1941.

EAST SURREYS' LIAISON WITH U.S. MARINES
Unit Which Called Here During Munich Crisis

(By A Special Correspondent.)

THE most pleasant memories that the East Surrey Regiment brings back from its 21 months tour in Shanghai, Tientsin and Peking is the very close liaison with the United States Marines.

It is very appreciative of the honour the Marines paid the Regiment when it "trooped" it out of Shanghai, its band heading the battalion as it made its farewell march through the International Settlement and into the Japanese concession to the docks for embarkation to Singapore.

It is not generally known that when the East Surreys were on their way to Shanghai in September, 1938, they arrived in Singapore on the day of the Munich crisis, and disembarked.

The battalion stayed in Tanglin for 12 days—until the crisis was over—and then sailed to Shanghai in another transport.

Double Duty

However, the next halt came at Hong Kong. It lasted four weeks, and it was not until the middle of November that the Battalion eventually arrived at Shanghai.

Like the Seaforth Highlanders, the East Surrey Regiment has had double duty to do in China.

In December last year, the reduction in the garrison in North China, saw a strong detachment being sent up to Tientsin, and this body remained there until it was ordered to move to Singapore.

Duties in Shanghai were "very heavy, with nothing exciting happening." The East Surreys were in the "Bad Lands District."

They mounted guard along the river with the Japanese on the other bank. They patrolled sectors, and maintained constant vigilance.

Although there was very little time for anything except duty because of the depleted numbers, the battalion raised soccer teams which this year won the junior league and were lead-

Lieut.-Col. G. E. Swinton, M.C., commanding officer of the East Surrey Regiment, now in Singapore.

battalions gained distinction in all theatres of war. Seven Victoria Crosses were awarded.

It was during the attack on Montauban, on the Somme, that the Eighth Battalion made history by advancing from the trenches to the attack, dribbling footballs.

On the capture of their objective, only one football was left, and this is now kept in the regimental museum at the Depot at Kingston.

We are greeted by the Straits Times upon our arrival from Shanghai, Sept. 1940.

Band practice under the rubber trees.

Off duty moments at the Chinese High School barracks, Bukit Timah Road, Singapore.

A Singapore street scene, 1941.

A country road in Malaya.

CHAPTER 4.

SINGAPORE FALLS.

Back at Penang that Tuesday 17th. December, exactly two years since I had set forth form Southampton, we feverishly loaded the small coastal steamer with our armaments. Most of our personal kit had to be left behind, each man being allowed just one haversack into which we crammed as much as possible.

By late afternoon we were ready and, accompanied by two of the Prai/Penang ferries, sailed out of the harbour. All three vessels were packed well above capacity and before we had reached the open sea one of the ferries began to sink, so its passengers had to be transferred to our boat, despite it being grossly overloaded. Next came the need to deny the stricken vessel to the pursuing enemy and a couple of rounds were fired from a small defensive gun mounted on our stern, which quickly despatched it to the bottom. By morning it had become obvious that the other ferry would not make it fully loaded and most of those aboard joined us too; a number of volunteers, including some sailor survivors from the sunken Prince of Wales and Repulse battleships, stayed and successfully sailed it into Port Swettenham further down the coast.

The decks were by now teeming with people, military personnel and civilians, the latter being mostly European women and children. The facilities for catering under these circumstances were very limited and we lived out of tins throughout the short voyage, during which Bob North and I manned a machine gun. It was mounted on a tripod located on the upper deck, pointing upwards awaiting the attack continuously expected, which blessedly never came. After two anxious days we arrived at Keppel Harbour in Singapore intact where, compared to our recent experiences, things seemed reasonably normal. But there had been considerable changes since my previous serene arrival in 1940, air raids of continuing intensity making their mark.

Upon disembarkation we assembled at No. 3 Mixed Reinforcement Camp in Braddell Road and after a few days most people left to rejoin their units. Before they departed Lindsay-Vears and I went along to the Hong Kong and Shanghai Bank and drew sufficient funds to make a final distribution of pay before Area Details disbanded. He now became attached to the staff of 2nd Echelon at Malaya Command and requested that I went with him. So began another phase under the guidance of that relentless 'gypsy'.

2nd Echelon was basically administrative, monitoring casualties and indenting for replacements. It carried out other duties but this was the section in which I now began to operate. Under the command of the Deputy Acting Adjutant General, staffing was solely by Indian Army personnel and I was duly transferred to the Indian Corps of Clerks with the rank of Sergeant. Our offices were located in the former St. Andrews School in Stamford Road, immediately down hill from Command Headquarters at Fort Canning, and I was soon working there busily typing cables for cyphers to transmit to the War Office in London. We were also responsible for the reporting of casualties to the Indian Army equivalent in New Delhi, code named Honour, and sometimes to the Australian War Department in Canberra. It was painful to learn the fate of my many friends from the stark, official forms sent in by their units.

Throughout that January, as the Japanese continued to advance down the Malay Peninsula, we became increasingly under attack by the same rigorous procedure of sorties carried out by groups of twenty-seven planes in three flights of nine. By now a limited number of early-type Hurricane fighters had arrived by sea crated and were hurriedly assembled but they proved to be no match for the more manoeuvrable Navy 'O's.

The few aircraft available were deplorable consisting, before the advent of the Hurricanes, of a small number of old planes such as the Brewster Buffalo, Blenheim Bomber and even 1920s vintage Wildebeest. The latter had a maximum speed of 100 miles per hour only and it took great courage for the Royal Air Force pilots to fly them in any circumstances, let alone in battle. They had my enduring admiration.

By the end of the month all of our forces had been withdrawn from the mainland and the battle for Singapore Island was about to begin. Artillery fire from the Japs in Johore across the Straits was now added to the air raids, which included machine gun strafing as well as high level pattern bombing; from our fire watching positions on the roof the falling bombs could be plainly seen. They produced a strange, horrendous beauty as they glistened in the brilliant sunshine.

After one week of frantic activity the enemy landed and from then onwards the cacophony of fighting was continuous. Soon we could hear the reports of the Japanese guns as they were fired and quickly learned to count the intervening seconds before the arrival of the shells. With more and more of them landing in the vicinity it was deemed prudent to evacuate the upstairs quarters where we were working and a makeshift office was prepared in the school hall downstairs; using ammunition boxes as desks and chairs we continued churning out our messages.

It was as well that we moved. The very next day the upstairs were destroyed by shellfire.

A few miles along the road furious fighting was raging, the British Battalion again being heavily involved in the same Bukit Timah area where we had trained after our arrival from Shanghai. Down at the docks some reinforcements, two brigades of the 18th Division under Major-General Beckwith-Smith, somewhat belatedly landed. They had been at sea for two months, were completely unacclimatised with no jungle training and, having lost most of their equipment when one of the ships in the convoy was set ablaze and sunk, were to be of limited help.

Black Friday the 13th February, 1942 commenced with the alert sounding in the early hours and from this time on we were embroiled in an inferno. The screech of roaring planes, the explosion of bombs, the whistle of shellfire - at least this would mean if one heard the sound of the shell it had passed overhead - coming from land and sea alike; all these things engulfed us. To add to the mayhem the oil tanks fired in denial created a huge black pall, and fires raged everywhere.

At Alexander Military Hospital an enormous atrocity was taking place. On the excuse that some Indian troops had fired on them from within the grounds, the Japanese Imperial Guards entered the hospital and immediately massacred all of the patients on the ground and first floors. Bursting into the operating theatre they slaughtered everyone with exception of one of the surgeons, Major Smythe, who feigned death when he was bayoneted. Most of the medical orderlies who had not been working in the wards at the time were rounded up and herded into a building for a day, after which they were marched away for mass execution. The bodies of the dead remained where they had fallen for the three days until capitulation. Only then was permission given for burial. After the war General Yamashita, the commander of the invading Japanese Army, was tried for the responsibility of this crime, found to be guilty and subsequently hung in Singapore.

On this same awful day, it having become obvious that the end was in sight, a decision was made to evacuate certain key personnel. A number were to be selected from 2nd. Echelon and Major Martin, the officer in charge of our section, visited the desk I had been sharing with Sergeant Bannister and said that one of us would be going. He finally decided it was only fair that as Bannister was the senior then he should be the one to go and so, to my then extreme disappointment, he was chosen. After hurriedly packing, he joined the remainder of the departing party who were assembling to leave for the docks; little did we realise as we waved them goodbye that it would be forever. Poor Bannister, their ship was attacked immediately it entered Singapore Roads and he perished with many others including yet another of my ex-Nevasa colleagues, Blondie Howell.

My star continued to wax amongst the many wanes.

In the meantime we carried on sending our messages although information coming in from the field was, to say the least, spasmodic. One day we were staggered to receive an admonitory cable from Honour, New Delhi stating:- "YOUR DIFFICULTIES APPRECIATED BUT PLEASE EXPEDITE". This surely was the understatement of the year. As mayhem raged around us we sadly reflected that the sender would no doubt be spending a pleasant evening in his peaceful Mess and then going back to his billet for a quiet night's sleep!

So the horror ground relentlessly on. All through that terrible Friday, right on during the night into Saturday and then with no relief to Sunday the barrage continued with ever increasing density. Unknown to us preliminary talks had been taking place between the opposing General Commanding Officers and we had no idea whatsoever that a ceasefire was imminent when a direct air attack was launched on us at 4.30 pm. I was busily typing away on the ammunition boxes facing the wall with main doors, both front and rear, wide open when there was the most terrifying, deafening explosion. The next thing I recall was shouting *"This is it!"* and diving by reflex action on to the concrete floor, my steel helmet flying away in the opposite direction. A hot blast circulated my limbs and as I gathered my wits I realized that the hall was densely thick with a haze of dust and rubble and that a huge fire was raging immediately outside the double front doors. Suddenly remembering that the room contained spare ammunition in our makeshift furniture we rapidly removed it out of the back doors away from the fire area, after which we had time to appraise the situation. How lucky I had been to escape unscathed! A whole stick of bombs had been dropped across our compound and a horrific scene greeted us, the huts on the other side of the drive about twenty feet away having been completely destroyed. Here had been housed the Indian Sepoys on detachment and all who were not on duty at the time suffered severe casualties, mostly killed. One of the bombs had fallen directly in their midst and we owed our lives to the open doors allowing the blast to pass right through our building without hindrance. This was the hot air experienced around our legs.

Other bombs had dropped just behind us and here there were more casualties, killed and wounded, to be attended to. Two of them were Indian cooks from the Sergeants Mess and as they were stretchered away one, badly wounded in the chest and bleeding profusely, apologized for not being able to complete 'Sahib's supper'. A valiant man. In the Stamford Road at the busy intersection just outside the entrance to the beleaguered Indian Quarters, a passing despatch rider had received the full impact of the explosion and all that remained of him were his burnt out motor cycle with his charred fingers still gripping the handlebars. The road, as had now become commonplace throughout the city, was strewn ankle deep. It was later discovered that we were even luckier than we had thought. Closer examination revealed that an unexploded bomb had in fact penetrated the building.

No more cables were despatched whilst we patiently waited. It seemed that the air raid was the final fling by the enemy and at 8.30pm the all-clear sounded for the first time since that fateful alert in the early hours of Friday. It was now the 15th February 1942, and we had capitulated.

The quietude was deafening.

CHAPTER 5.

INTO CAPTIVITY.

Exhausted as we were, no one slept on that fateful night. At one o'clock in the morning instructions came to hand in all arms in compliance with the terms of surrender and I parted with my first world war Lee Enfield rifle serial number 601, which had been my constant companion for the past two years. We stood around in groups earnestly discussing our plight and endeavouring to assess the future - the Japanese reputation for the treatment of their prisoners of war in China and Hong Kong not being of the highest order.

Batches of stragglers who had become separated from their units drifted into the compound during the night. One of them was a sailor survivor from HMS Prince of Wales who regaled us with tales of his adventures which among other things included serving under Lord Louis Mountbatten on HMS Kelly and escaping when that too was lost earlier in the war. Together with the other naval and marine survivors from sunken vessels he had been fighting as an infantryman, making up a force with the remains of the Argyll & Sutherland Highlanders who, like the East Surreys, had fought long and valiantly the whole way down the peninsula. The mixed unit proudly called themselves the 'Plymouth Highlanders'.

By daybreak we began to see Japanese cars driving by making for the adjacent Command HQ at Fort Canning, where the hated 'fried egg' flag was now flying. There was, though, still no sign of their troops.

We pondered on what to do for the immediate present and the nineteen of us comprising the permanent staff decided that it might be prudent to make some provision for the days ahead, so a party left at once for the docks to see what they could find. Many others were on a similar missions but our chaps quickly found a truck and were soon loading it with stocks of tinned food from one of the godowns. In addition to this valuable load they also picked up a tea chest full of Victory 'V' cigarettes and then hurriedly drove back. These acquisitions were to be of great benefit in the months to come.

Sergeant Cameron, a fiery Scot, had decided overnight to try getting away and left in search of a boat. His fate is unknown. The rest of us received instructions on Tuesday, 17th, to march the fourteen miles out to the same Changi where we had been encamped eighteen months earlier. As our captors had no means of provisioning us in the immediate future they permitted the use of a limited number of loaded trucks, which had to be returned to Tyersall Park, Tanglin, the next morning. We were thus able to take our newly gained 'prize'. Lindsay-Vears did not come as, due to his age and being a local resident, he was advised to revert to his civilian status. All non military Europeans had to report to Changi Jail - the many criminal prisoners having already been released - where they were interned and he joined them. I have neither seen nor heard of him since.

So we became part of the long, winding column of thousands proceeding along the stricken, sorry streets. The signs of battle were everywhere, the local population of the normally teeming city being conspicuous by their absence. Japanese road blocks abounded and before long we were passing many groups of their soldiers riding the bicycles that were a feature of transport in the enemy campaign. As they went by I ruefully recalled that a survey of cycle riders was conducted at Tanjong Pau soon after we originally arrived there but no machines were ever issued or indeed any of the non-riders taught. The cycles, infuriatingly, were available but never left the stores down at Tanjong Malim until the Japs arrived there and helped themselves to the welcome find.

On we trudged along the East Coast Road, alas no longer serene, up and down the hilly roads until reaching the padang opposite the same Roberts Barracks of previous acquaintance. Resting here at the former guardroom one of my marching companions, Captain Russell-Roberts, and I discovered several large stone jars filled with rum which we quickly commandeered. Carefully rationed the find provided vital nourishment over the next few difficult weeks.

The captain's wife, a strikingly attractive and popular lady, had also been employed in our office as a secretary until a week before the end when she left on one of the official evacuation parties. Surviving her vessel's shipwreck, she was captured and imprisoned on Banka Island in Indonesia. This place was plagued by a mysterious fever and sadly she was one of the many who succumbed in 1944.

Our journey ended at Fairy Point House where General Percival and the whole of Command HQ were already installed. It was obvious that there would be insufficient room for us all and after a day or two of literally milling about we moved into the roofless squash courts across the road. The Japanese had made it quite clear that they would not be in a position to issue any rations for at least ten days so, in response to a general appeal, we deposited the contents of our lorry load with the Royal Army Service Corps. Other groups made similar contributions which enabled the establishment of a distribution centre, thereby ensuring restricted food supplies for all.

We kept the cigarettes though!

The whole of Changi was teeming, every building and shack including the now empty shops in the village being occupied. Organization of the vast camp areas was left to our own authorities, the Australians taking over Selarang Barracks and the British settling in the Roberts, India and Kitchener areas. In all there were some 50,000 troops, which except for the British officers did not include the Indians. They were separated and detained in their own camps in Singapore, mainly at Tanglin, where they soon came under pressure to enlist in the so-called Free Indian Army to fight alongside the enemy. Regrettably a considerable number, mainly Sikhs, did so but the faithful Gurkhas refused to a man.

The already crowded conditions worsened when room had to be found shortly afterwards for the wounded who had been left behind in Singapore at the Alexandra and General Hospitals. Roberts Barracks was cleared and converted into a hospital to accommodate them and remained in this capacity for the remainder of the war.

First and foremost sanitation exercised our minds and at once many boreholes were speedily dug for latrines and Otway pits constructed for the disposal of refuse. Nevertheless it was not long before dysentery was rife, swelling the ranks of the already over burdened hospital and the newly established cemetery.

During these early days there was a bonus inasmuch as we were able to roam wherever one wished and at this time we could even bathe or fish in the pagar at Fairy Point. After about a month, though, orders were received for the various areas to be wired in. To reach the Australians at Selarang, the 18th Division at India Barracks or the Southern Area where the Surreys were, it was necessary to cross under a special flag carried by one of our own officers. It was all quite strange, we rarely set eyes on any Japs, and I am sorry to record that the inter-joining roads traversed by the flag parties were patrolled by Sikhs who had transferred their allegiance. They frequently assaulted us for the slightest imagined misdemeanour, especially singling out any Indian Army officers whom they recognized.

Fairy Point House under construction 1928.

At this time we were evicted from Fairy Point, the Japs no doubt not wishing us to see any more of the stricken ships of their navy passing through the Johore Straits. Our new quarters were some five hundred yards along Fairy Point Road at Temple Hill, on the top of which the former Royal Engineers Officers Mess building was located, in the remains of a wooden hut way down the perimeter road which in peace time had housed Mess staff. Extensively damaged by shell fire, only three sections remained but we soon

The Bathing Pagar at Fairy Point.

made a reasonable home for the nineteen of us and at least it was an improvement on the concrete floor of the squash courts and did provide a roof over our heads.

We even managed to construct some BEDS. When the truck had been returned to Tanglin it went back, at Sergeant Filby's suggestion, minus a large tarpaulin it contained. Cutting the green material into sections and using timber and nails taken from demolished parts of the hut to make the frames over which it was stretched, we soon had a comfortable bed apiece. Who said that necessity was not the mother of invention?

The daily diet of rice, eight ounces per man supplemented by meagre supplies of meat of dubious quality, not only left one hungry but took some time to adjust to. Most people became severely constipated, it being quite common to experience periods of ten to fourteen days between motions, but in due course more normal movement returned as our bodies accepted the drastic change. In fact for many the opposite happened and bacillary dysentery persisted despite the strenuous sanitation measures. Everybody became fly conscious - as big a menace as the Japs - and we all made fly swats, never to be without.

Lack of vitamin B2 produced unpleasant scourges, the most common of which was persistent irritation of the scrotum. Even more uncomfortable were the sore mouths, tongues and throats making eating food very painful. To combat these early symptoms of avitaminosis, the forerunner of beriberi, the doctors were exploring sources of the essential vitamin. It is contained in peanuts, very few of which could be obtained, and the yeast that was extracted from rice husks which again was very limited. What had come to light, though, were considerably large stocks of fish meal fertilizer and, after tests proved that it was rich in B2, it was distributed for consumption. This was simply foul but everyone forced it down each day until supplies ran out. To help, our inventive cooks soon found a method of baking the mess in the form of flat cakes which made it just about digestible.

These same cooks, volunteers all of them, under the supervision of some regular cook house personnel, had quickly mastered the art of bulk rice cooking in open kwalies - a cast iron bowl about three feet in diameter of ten gallon capacity which devotees of Chinese cuisine would recognize as a type of big kwok.

Valuable stocks of the English Marmite and Australian Vegemite, vegetable yeast extract rich in the same vitamin, were also discovered and carefully husbanded by the hospital administration. A spoonful per day issued to those suffering badly enough to need medical treatment worked wonders.

To vary the monotonous three times per day rice diet a type of flour was produced. This entailed grinding the grains, initially by rolling on a flat surface with bottles but later with grinding machines made up by the Royal Engineers. Now we could enjoy a form of rice 'bread', just a small piece with the evening meal, whilst for breakfast imitation porridge evolved by browning before grinding and then cooking into a pappy condition. Our one dessert spoonful of sugar, issued on alternating days, made it quite palatable.

Lunch consisted of plain boiled rice and in the evening, the main meal of the day, the fare was half a mess tin of yet more rice with a little meat plus the obligatory fertilizer cake. It was all washed down with a drink of tea minus, of course, any milk or sugar. In these early days I had money, some 150 Straits Dollars left over from my last pay day and was able, through the medium of working parties now visiting the docks in the city, to make purchases of extra titbits that were obtainable in the already flourishing black market.

Thus on Whitsuntide Monday Ron Wells and I were in the enviable position of enjoying the luxury of sharing a tin of pilchards in tomato sauce. Sheer nectar!

Shortly after settling in at Temple Hill another of our number, Sergeant Oliver, decided to try escaping. Having served in Singapore since 1938 he knew the country very well and was confident of crossing to the mainland, obtaining a boat and sailing it to Ceylon. So he bravely departed and after hearing nothing for sometime we began to think that he had succeeded until one day an ominous report was circulated. It stated that a British soldier was in hospital in Changi - suffering from alleged shark wounds, after being rescued from the sea. In the general opinion it was believed that this was a cover up story for an escapee who had been caught and had been injured by sword blows. We never heard the final outcome.

Our daily routine continued with sanitation duties and the cleansing of monsoon gullies in preventative malarial measures, tasks shared with staff of 3rd Corps Headquarters. They too were members of the Indian Corps of Clerks who were billeted in another bomb damaged hut further round the hill. Also at the bottom of the hill, with whom we shared a mutual kitchen, were a Royal Signals unit and amongst them I found an old school friend, Danny Treacher. I don't know who was the most surprised.

During this period the Japanese continued to leave us to our own devices and, most units now having reassembled in their original formations, military discipline was re-imposed with regular drill parades and physical exercises. During leisure hours many social activities evolved, including a quite unique educational organization which became known as the 'Changi University' where it was possible to enrol in a wide diversity of subjects for tuition by a wealth of intellectual talent. For the less diligent, numerous professional and keen amateur entertainers initiated a series of concerts produced at the open air cinema in Changi village and at the modern army cinema building at Roberts Barracks. A particularly memorable show at the former venue was an ambitious production called 'Hellzapoppin', starring Jack McNaughton, who was a member of a distinguished theatrical family, and Captain 'Fizzer' Pearson. We were to be entertained many times in the future by the inimitable Fizzer, a gifted amateur. The Australians had also formed concert parties and they had an excellent comedian, who would perform on stilts and had gained universal acclaim for his droll 'We'll never get off this Island' catchphrase. Travelling players, they came and performed for us at Temple Hill on the raised entrance porch of the former Officers' Mess. In this same building we found solace on Sunday evenings listening to a recital of symphony music, courtesy of a young officer who had located an old wind up gramophone and quite a good selection of records - goodness knows where from. The original Mess Library was still intact from which reading material was made available and so, apart from being constantly hungry and having to put up with a chronic shortage of water, conditions were bearable.

The entrance to the Southern Area was not very far away and I often took the 'man ferry' through no-mans land to visit my friends in the East Surreys, who were located in the Changi village area. They had received a severe mauling in the campaign and were very reduced in numbers. The original strength of the Leicestershires and themselves had been about 700 in each battalion, but when they were reformed at Ipoh the combined unit could muster only 786; at Mount Echo, where they finally laid down their arms on 15th February, they had been reduced to just 265. Some were to turn up later from Northern Malaya, where they had been held at Kuala Lumpur since the capture after the earlier fighting, but many had been lost. In another accolade Lt. General Sir Lewis Heath, the General Officer Commanding 3rd Corps recorded that "The British Battalion, despite casualties which would have shattered the morale of any unit not imbued with grandest spirit, magnificently officered and led, continued to fight on solidly and undismayed till the very end".

Len, I was pleased to see, was in fine heart and Ches, although still suffering from the effects of a nasty gun shot wound in his shoulder, was again butchering in the cookhouse. He had had a narrow escape at Alexander Hospital, having been a patient on the top floor at the time of the massacre. Apart from Harry Wise, I was unable to locate any of the lads from the 2/6th contingent - all of them having already left on working parties for other destinations.

It was even possible to indulge in some light hearted cricket on the padang, instigated by Captain Ben Barnett, an Australian Test player who had toured England in both 1934 and 1938, and Major E. W. Swanton, the latter being a well-known cricket writer and commentator. But changes were taking place, large parties having moved out to a camp in River Valley Road to work in the docks and others, including Bob Deane, had left for Japan, Borneo and

Thailand. In June all officers above the rank of Lieutenant Colonel were sent to camps established for high ranking officers in Korea and Manchuria.

These moves had not yet affected our group and we continued much as the before but had now become involved in the felling of coconut trees for fuel purposes. This entailed manhandling trailers to bring in the felled timbers, which were in fact army trucks minus engines that had been stripped to the chassis. We pulled them up and down the hills with ropes and it proved to be a considerable skill to negotiate the steep slopes. It was positively hair-raising descending, depending very much on who was at the steering wheel. Water, always in short supply, was delivered to central points in each area by the same method in petrol-less water wagons.

It was a strange experience, this being cut off from the world. When I visited Tony Clifton-Griffith, my companion at Penang, at the ration stores where he now worked near Changi Hill, I would stay awhile on my own at the stump of Changi Tree. The tree had long been a landmark but had been lopped during the campaign to clear the firing line for the large 15" guns, which had been turned round from their fixed positions to fire at the Japanese on the mainland. Unfortunately the ammunition was armour piercing for attacking ships and did not prove to be very effective. It was here that I sat on a prominent part of the hill looking out to sea, reflecting when and how on earth we would extricate ourselves. The ocean seemed so vast and home so far away.

With the arrival of August the men from Nippon started to make their presence more obvious. Major-General Fukuye had taken command of the prisoner of war organization and immediately ordered that all must sign a statement worded:-

"*I, the undersigned, hereby solemnly swear on my honour that I will not, under any circumstances, attempt to escape*".

This was tantamount to giving our parole and the orders were immediately protested. The senior British officer, Lt. Colonel Holmes of the Manchester Regiment and his counterpart with the Australians, Lt. Colonel Gallaghan, argued strongly that under our military regulations this was not permitted. Accordingly not a single man signed.

Nothing more was heard from Fukuye for a couple of days but then he reacted violently.

Changi Tree, also showing (in the background on the right), Roberts Barracks.

Aerial view of Roberts Barracks, Changi.

Selarang Incident, September 1942.

CHAPTER 6.

SELARANG.

On the 2nd September, 1942 orders were received for everybody, except the most serious hospital patients, to move into Selarang Barracks. These were situated about two miles from Temple Hill and comprised seven of the same two storey concrete blocks as elsewhere in Changi; it was the former home of the 1st Battalion Gordon Highlanders and designed to accommodate 900 men. Into this area which, when calculating the space taken on the ground and two upper floors plus the flat roofs, was approximately seven acres we crammed 15,400 British and Australians. Room also had to be found for our cooking appertances and the remainder of our sparse possessions. About 2,000 had remained behind in Roberts Hospital.

We joined the general exodus trekking through the deep valley which separated the Roberts complex and Selarang, carrying as much as possible of our limited equipment. Regretfully the home made beds had to be left at Temple Hill. Upon arrival it was found that all the accommodation in the buildings had been taken, so we settled down in the open on the tarmacadam parade ground surrounded by the seven barrack blocks. There were three on one side, two on the other and two at one end with administration blocks making up the square at the other end. There were no toilet facilities, the few lavatories in the buildings being totally inadequate and the Japs had in any case cut off the water supply to the cisterns which were gravity fed from tanks on the roofs. To meet this need, rotating working parties immediately commenced breaking up the tarmacadam surface and its concrete base in the centre of the square and then, with the aid of the faithful augurs, dug several rows of bore holes. The augurs were actually shovels bolted together on a central bar with another one affixed horizontally and operated by four men walking around in a circle. The carpenters did what they could to construct seating of sorts, known as 'thunderboxes', but of course there was no privacy whatsoever and soon the whole place was infested with flies. My call to work on the operation came during the middle of the night.

The water supply was provided by just two taps, one on either side of the compound, where continuous queues formed to collect the one water bottle per man allowed each day which had to suffice for all purposes including drinking, cooking and washing. No rations at all were issued on the first day but on the second a limited amount of rice was allocated; in dozens of makeshift kitchens the cooks did their best to provide some sort of sustenance. We were encircled by a perimeter road, patrolled by both Japanese troops and Indians from the 'Indian National Army', the former manning machine guns at strategic positions and it was made plain that anybody venturing into the road would be regarded as escaping and would be shot on the spot. We settled in to make the best of things, despite being absolutely soaked on the first evening by one of Singapore's sudden tropical downpours - the ferocity of which has to be experienced to be believed. Undaunted by events, as night fell a platform was magically erected in the midst of that sea of humanity on which some of our entertainers performed an impromptu concert. It was not long before the thousands of determined men were lustily singing 'There'll always be an England', 'Waltzing Matilda' and many other popular songs, concluding with the National Anthem. The Japanese just stood and gazed in puzzled amazement. The next day a series of meetings took place between our senior officers and Fukuye, when he threatened to stop all food supplies, but everybody remained adamant in their refusal to sign. An even more sinister incident then arose.

In the preceding months a few others had followed our friend Oliver's example and made an attempt to escape. Four of them, two Australian and two British, had gone off independently but all were caught up country and after interrogation returned to their respective units. A number of days previously they had been re-arrested, one being taken from his hospital bed, and now Colonels Holmes and Galleghan were conveyed to Changi Beach and informed that all four had been denied any trial and would be executed in their presence. On arrival the tragic, courageous men were made to dig their own graves before facing the firing squad, which I regret to record contained some Sikhs. Their aim was very ragged and accordingly the victims were not even allowed a clean death. One of the British was Private Waters of the East Surreys, popularly known throughout the battalion as 'Shag'. He was one of a hard core of regular soldiers who were the backbone of the army who during the campaign had showed extreme bravery and leadership, being of invaluable help to some of the less experienced officers and N.C.O.s. Shag was something of an eccentric. At Tanjong Pau, for instance, to relieve the boredom he acquired some chickens for whom he built a small chicken run adjacent to his hut. Even Colonel Swinton had to smile at this initiative. Before they were shot down Corporal Breavington, one of the Australians, pleaded that his companion was ordered by him to escape and therefore he alone should be punished. It was to no avail and the final action of the victims was to stand to attention and salute their commanding officers.

Just retribution came in April, 1946 when a War Crimes sitting in Singapore sentenced Fukuye to death and he was duly executed.

An unknown author, a compatriot of Corporal Breavington, wrote this tribute:-

THE CORPORAL AND HIS PAL.

He stood, a dauntless figure
Prepared to meet his fate.
Upon his lips a kindly smile,
One arm about his mate;
His free hand held a picture
Of the one he loved most dear
And though the hand was trembling
It was not caused by fear.
No braver man e'er faced his death
Before a firing squad
That stood that day upon the square
And placed his trust in God.
He drew himself up proudly
And faced the leering foe,
His rugged face grew stern: "I ask
One favour e're I go.
Grant unto me this last request
That's in your power to give.
For myself I ask no mercy

But let my comrade live".
Then turning to the guardhouse
Where his sad-faced Colonel stands
A witness to his pending fate
Brought here by Jap command.
He stiffened to attention
His hand swings up on high
To hat brim, in a swift salute,
"I'm ready now to die".
They murdered him in hatred
And prolonged his tortured end.
In spite of all his pleadings
They turned and shot his friend.
They said it was an example
Of what they had in store
For others who tried to escape
Whilst Prisoner of War.
Example, yes - of how to die,
And how to meet one's fate.
Example, true - of selfless love
A man has for his mate.
And when he reaches Heaven's Gate
The Angels will be nigh,
And welcome in their midst a man
Who knew the way to die.
Whilst here below in letters gold,
The scroll of fame e'er shall
The story tell of how they died,
A Corporal and his Pal.

Sickness in the confined area was inevitably spreading, with the ever present dysentery and now some cases of the diphtheria that had already been raising its ugly head and threatening to become of epidemic proportions. Notwithstanding, no patients were allowed to be sent back to the hospital and on the third day the first death occurred. On this very same day Fukuye issued an ultimatum; unless we agreed to sign at once the whole of the inmates in Roberts Hospital would be moved in to join the rest of us. Although we all remained prepared to stand firm, the two commanders advised that as complying with this latest cruel instruction could mean hundreds of men losing their lives - a step they felt could not be taken - a joint directive was made advising we sign under duress. Both officers would accept full responsibility for us thus breaking 'King's Regulations'. And so, on the morning of the 5th September, the hated pieces of paper were circulated which we queued up to sign, after which everybody returned to their former quarters throughout Changi.

It was not to be my final association with Selarang.

Upon arrival at Temple Hill we found our makeshift beds intact, after all there was no one about to interfere as everybody had been incarcerated. The return was short lived for within a couple of weeks we were uprooted again and relocated in, of all places, that same Selarang Barracks. This time it really was good-bye to the beds, lack of transport for conveyance obliging us to leave them behind. Occupying the ground floor of one of the blocks at the southern end, we were not so overcrowded but had to re-adapt to sleeping on the concrete floor. The lavatories though had been reconnected, which was a bonus.

My initial cash had long since evaporated so there were few chances of buying extras in the black market, itself on the wane as supplies in Singapore dried up and the absence of any working parties travelling to and fro eliminated contacts. My last source of income was the sale of some of my Victory 'V' cigarettes - we had 1000 each - but that too had now come to an end. One commodity that could still be purchased were the vitamin rich peanuts and I looked round for ways of earning a few extra dollars to help me ward off the avitaminosis, especially as the fertilizer rations had stopped. In the next block was a large, gangling officer who in happier times had been Judge Advocate in Thailand and when I heard that he was looking for someone to do his laundry I swallowed my pride and volunteered. The only other defence against the lack of B2 was a vile tasting yeast drink made by fermenting rice husks, not always available as sometimes only polished rice was issued. In fact, due to chronic shortages during this period, we received some that had been stored for many years in lime which turned into a horrible yellow, gooey mess upon cooking. It required much discipline to consume. The overall diet was deteriorating, there being very little fresh meat or vegetables and the occasional yam or dried fish was a treat.

Not surprisingly the conditions were beginning to take their toll. Diarrhoea was commonplace and dysentery had become more widespread, whilst diphtheria, relishing the overcrowding, reached epidemic proportions. In addition malaria, which had been virtually eliminated under British rule, returned despite our own efforts to keep the drains and monsoon gullies free of stagnation. The Japs failed to carry out any preventative measures whatsoever, which was to be a feature in all territories under occupation. Most of the deaths in the early months had been battle wounded who had failed to recover in the primitive conditions, but now they were being the result of malnutrition and disease. Beriberi had also arisen but was not yet the scourge it was to become later.

Fortunately I avoided incurring, at this stage, nothing worse than an uncomfortable period with pellagra causing the discomfort of sore lips, mouth and throat - though the peanuts that I was able to purchase soon cleared it up.

Some were still fit enough to play a little football on a makeshift pitch at the back of our block, across that very same road covered by Jap machine gun posts during the recent 'Selarang Incident'. Signalman Nash, the despatch rider from Penang, proved to be a star centre-forward and scored several goals in a hastily arranged England versus Scotland match. One of the participants in this game, Gunner Halliwell, was dead within three weeks from dysentery - an indication of the deteriorating conditions.

Tree-felling continued and the open areas created used for gardens, the papayas and sweet potatoes grown there eventually becoming a vital part of the diet of those who remained in Changi. On one occasion Bill Threlful badly gashed his thigh with an axe and was admitted to hospital. His absence reduced our numbers and, with Sergeants Filby and Collins electing to return to their original units, we were now down to fourteen.

Being without any outside contact, rumour upon rumour abounded as they had in fact ever since capture. It had not been long before secret home made radios were operating but, as the penalty for such action was almost certainly death, utmost security was essential. The technique adopted was for the listeners to withhold any firm news for at least three weeks and then release it mixed with invented stories. Circulation by word of mouth normally took place at the latrines and became known as 'bore hole rumours'. One such, the most persistent, was that negotiations had taken place with the Portuguese and that we were to be moved to an internment camp in Lourenco- Marques under neutral supervision! In fact, the story went, the vessels that would take us had already sailed for Singapore with repatriated Japanese diplomats aboard. It transpired that ships did arrive from South Africa bringing them back, but not to collect us.

Nobody really believed this fanciful tale but good did come in the form of Red Cross supplies, the first of the only two occasions this was to happen - the second taking place in 1944. There were no individual parcels, the supplies being in bulk and consisting of foodstuffs and some clothing. The former, tinned meat and vegetables plus tomato jam and cocoa, were added to the ration stores for distribution whilst the limited clothing had to be allocated by ballot. I was not one of the lucky ones. Most people who were seemed only to receive a 'pork pie' type trilby hat, but as I still had my bush hat it did not really matter. There were some socks though that would have been most welcome.

The majority of us had lost nearly all our kit during the campaign and my total inventory was:-

    2 off vests.
    2 prs. underpants.
    2 shirts.
    1 pr. shorts.
    1 pr. long khaki drill trousers.
    1 pr. socks.
    1 pr. boots.
    1 bush hat.
    razor, toothbrush and 1 towel.

At no time did our 'hosts' provide clothing of any kind and, living in uncivilized conditions in a tropical climate, what we did have soon began to wear out. Soap was at a premium for washing and we conserved it and our meagre supply of razor blades by shaving only on alternate days. When the blades had all gone, we learned that a stainless steel table knife sharpened up excellently and was a good substitute.

In October most of the working parties in Singapore had departed up country and similar groups were being assembled in Changi. The actual destination was Thailand and the Japanese stated that the transfer would be to specially constructed camps in a region where better food supplies were more readily available. We were even encouraged to take as many of the light sick as possible because the improved conditions would help in their recovery and this was generally believed. We should have known better. Each party was some 700 strong and came from all quarters, which entailed the breaking up of established formations; on 2nd November we joined one such group, the Royal Signals who had been our companions since Temple Hill coming with us. Some of our fourteen 2nd Echelon staff stayed behind, among them being the senior Warrant Officer, Bill Morrell, due to his age. He was approaching fifty.

Boarding a convoy of trucks, we left for Singapore railway station. On the way we passed the notorious Changi Jail and were greeted by the civilian internees, who waved from the various windows. The station was swarming with Japs when we arrived and lined up to board the train. Our carriages were enclosed steel goods wagons measuring twelve feet by six, into which we crowded thirty-two men plus all of their equipment. It at once became obvious that a cargo had recently been unloaded, as we found to our discomfort as we squeezed into our tight positions. The metal floor was strewn with messy oil stained straw. Our journey into Hell had begun.

CHAPTER 7.

DESTINATION KWAI.

Jammed into the wagons like sardines, it was most uncomfortable and, with the sun beating down unmercifully on the metal roof, so very, very hot. Just the one haversack carried all of my kit but some officers who had remained in Singapore during the campaign came with more bulk, including a number of bedrolls; room also had to be found for medical and cooking equipment. There being literally insufficient space to lie prone, everyone took turns to sit in the middle beside the open door on the near side. So we set forth, with no water or food to sustain us.

Progress was monumentally slow and, as the day extended, I began to wonder if we were ever going to stop. With the majority suffering from varying degrees of diarrhoea and all with rice-orientated weak bladders, the calls of nature soon presented a problem. This brought the need for people to relieve themselves from the moving train, their companions who happened to be sitting near the door acting as 'anchors' - our degradation thereby reaching new lows. On and on we buffeted, the heat becoming ever more intense and I never imagined it possible to perspire so much, we were all simply drenched. Relief finally came at Gemas, some 200 miles distant, where we stopped and alighted to receive the first meal of the day, cold sour rice and a drink of tea. The tea was the usual large leaf variety, the standard issue at all times, which we had by now become accustomed to drinking without embellishment *(at Selarang, though, we discovered that brewing it with the locally grown lalang grass produced a pleasant lemon flavour)*. At Gemas, as at all the other stops en route, no lavatories were available and all had to suffer the further indignity of defecating alongside of the track.

Moving on again into the night little progress was made as we shunted back and forth in a number of sidings, leaving the main track clear to make way for military traffic. Now thankfully spared the torture of the sun, it was still very humid but at least the movement of the train kept the swarming mosquitoes at bay. Even so, it was too uncomfortable to rest for long and, having only slept fitfully, I was not sorry when daybreak arrived with us pulling into the magnificent Kuala Lumpur station. Despite the grim surroundings one could still appreciate the grandeur of its British Victorian architecture - akin to a cathedral with minarets.

Breakfast, it was to suffice for the rest of that second day, was the normal plain, cold rice plus a piece of dehydrated fish which was a particular 'delicacy' known to all and sundry as 'stinkfish'. Continuing on our way through familiar country, the journey was proving to be a far cry from that experienced when the East Surreys moved up to Tanjong Pau nearly two years previously. Another long, unpleasant day took us through the tin mining areas with its huge white slag heaps near Ipoh until, following another night of bumping and boring, arriving at Prai. Here I could see the lovely island of Penang quite clearly and must say I sighed for the halcyon days of my six months spent there the previous year, wondering to myself what on earth it was like across in Georgetown now. No doubt the Japs were installed in the excellent Glugor Cantonment, which I had described in a letter to home as being easily the best barracks in the world! Next we creaked, groaned and crawled to Alor Star, from which station we had so proudly marched off from in the past. Now some of us were back, ragged and ashamed. My morale, though, did receive a boost when I espied an Indian civilian railwayman on the platform hiding behind a shed out of sight of the guards. I had just returned to the train from our usual unedifying break to await departure and as we left he stood, with tears in his eyes and hands put together in the traditional form of greeting, saying *"British Raj, please come back"*.

A surprise was the change in the new Siamese border, which had been moved down to encompass the States of Kedah and Perlis. Thailand had for long cherished the return of this territory and the annexation was a sop from the Japanese, part of the bargain agreed for declaring war on the Allies. It made no difference at all, as the Japs occupied both countries, the Thais only being their puppets.

Thailand. Now we really were entering into the unknown. Soon the countryside started to change considerably with the peninsular area in the south, which was rice bearing, consisting of seemingly endless miles of padi fields. The ever present water buffaloes, with whom we had already become acquainted during the days on manoeuvres in Kedah, were much in evidence - little did we think then that they would provide invaluable meat rations. Stops became more frequent and, there not being so much control by our guards over the local population, it was possible to trade at some of the stations. So we sold some of our sparse valuables and purchased bananas, duck eggs and cigarettes; some, with nothing of value to trade parted with shirts off their backs. It was a rash thing to do, which many came to regret later, but hungry people tend to act irrationally. I haggled with a Thai for the sale of my wristwatch, which to be honest was not a very good one, that had long since stopped working properly due to the humidity of the tropics. The deal was for a hand of bananas and some cigarettes and, knowing the poor quality of my product, I waited until the train was slowly moving out before concluding the transaction. Judging by his cries as he ran along the platform he was not well pleased, especially when the glass fell out in his hand. I felt a bit guilty until opening the newspaper parcel containing the cigarettes and finding that half of them had been substituted by pieces of chalk! However, we all had a feast that alleviated our hunger and then a good smoke, chalk or not. It was a long time since we had been able to obtain any tobacco and back in Changi many had experimented in smoking cherry tree leaves. The cigarettes we had just acquired were a locally produced Virginia type called Red Bull and Sheaf, the latter being the slightly better quality.

Destination still unknown, we were in fact at the half way stage. So the journey ground relentlessly on until on the fifth day we came to a place called Ban Pong, which was a small town about fifty miles west of Bangkok. Unshaven, dirty and weary, we detrained and were marched off through the town towards this 'haven' that had been promised by our captors. Passing through the gates we found it simply appalling. At the time of our arrival the rainy season was approaching the end of its span, but had not yet eased, and the rain had been falling steadily as we had marched. Now we were greeted by a flooded transit camp which had been erected by people who had had the misfortune of being sent up earlier in June and had already moved on up country. They had started work on a railway to be built from Ban Pong to Moulmein in Burma, a distance of some 250 miles through fever infested country which was mountainous and mainly virgin jungle. It was rumoured that such a project had been surveyed some years earlier by a European consortium and had been rejected as too hazardous; this did not bother the Japanese, who had an expendable labour force.

Entering the camp, we found that it consisted of a series of long, low huts built entirely of bamboo and roofed with atap - a kind of palm frond. Each one was 200 feet long and there were no windows, just occasional openings for access, with the roof coming down to within inches of the ground. A bamboo platform, about two feet high, ran along the whole length on each side which provided sleeping accommodation on bamboo slats. The floor was just the bare earth and it was now flooded several inches deep from end to end. Everywhere was a quagmire. The open trench latrines - no such things as bore-hole augurs existed here - had overflowed and effluent abounded. Flies swarmed in their thousands and all in all it was not very pleasant or easy; these pests were constantly with us and food had to be eaten with as much protection as possible whilst beating them off with the inevitable fly-swat.

Ploughing through the wet morass, we lined up at the cook house and collected our first meal of any substance since leaving Changi. It was of course the customary rice and what was soon christened 'jungle stew', containing a hint of water buffalo meat with a concoction of locally grown vegetables. These were normally Chinese radish, pumpkin and bean shoots but on this occasion some tinned M&V from the recent Red Cross supplies had been added. From the same source came a once only drink of good old fashioned cocoa, a real treat especially as we were able to acquire some Gula Malacca - an indigenous molasses - to sweeten it.

The guards were Koreans under the command of Japanese officers and N.C.O.s who, with just a few isolated exceptions, proved to be as cruel and sadistic as their masters. They had a voracious appetite for watches, fountain pens and cigarette lighters and were soon indicating a desire to trade but it was unwise to indulge them. The amounts they were prepared to pay were low and haggling often meant a blow to the head and possible confiscation if anyone possessed a Rolex watch, Parker pen or Ronex lighter. These latter products, we learned in due course when trading contacts had been established with Thais, fetched considerably higher prices than any other type. It was quite common at this time to see Koreans with a whole row of watches strapped to their arms, which they no doubt sold to the local population at a profit.

Thankfully, we moved on from this Godforsaken place after

just two days to Kanchanaburi, familiarly called Kanburi, a small but important town forty miles distant. Situated in a delta where the River Mae Khlong joins the River Khwae Noi, it was here that the Japanese engineers supervising the railway construction had established their headquarters. Travelling in a convoy of open trucks and tightly packed in standing positions, it was a hair raising ride, the Jap drivers proving to be very erratic, but we got there in one piece. In fact we were extremely lucky to go by truck, later parties coming up from Changi had to march.

Our rendezvous was an old grassed aerodrome whose only claim to fame was the landing there in 1930 of Amy Johnson, on her epic solo flight from England to Australia. She would have found difficulty now because, as at Ban Pong, it was completely flooded. Assembling on the perimeter, we sloshed through the water several inches deep until reaching some bell tents, which were pitched on slightly higher ground. Inside it was found that the flood was only peripheral and there was sufficient dry ground around the tent pole, where we deposited our belongings and made our wet way to collect a meal. To return with the food without mishap was very tricky, balancing two halves of a mess tin through the water with the slippery surface below requiring much concentration. Some unfortunates went flying, it was already night time, losing their rations but their tent companions shared with them and no one went to sleep completely hungry. Such close comradeship was a consoling feature of our existence.

Afterwards we huddled in sitting positions on our dry 'island', much as we had on the train journey, and slept to the best of our ability. At sunrise the wet trek to the cook-house was repeated, this time thankfully in daylight so there were not so many disasters. That morning we were on our way yet once again. Oh gypsy, gypsy, what were you doing to me?

64

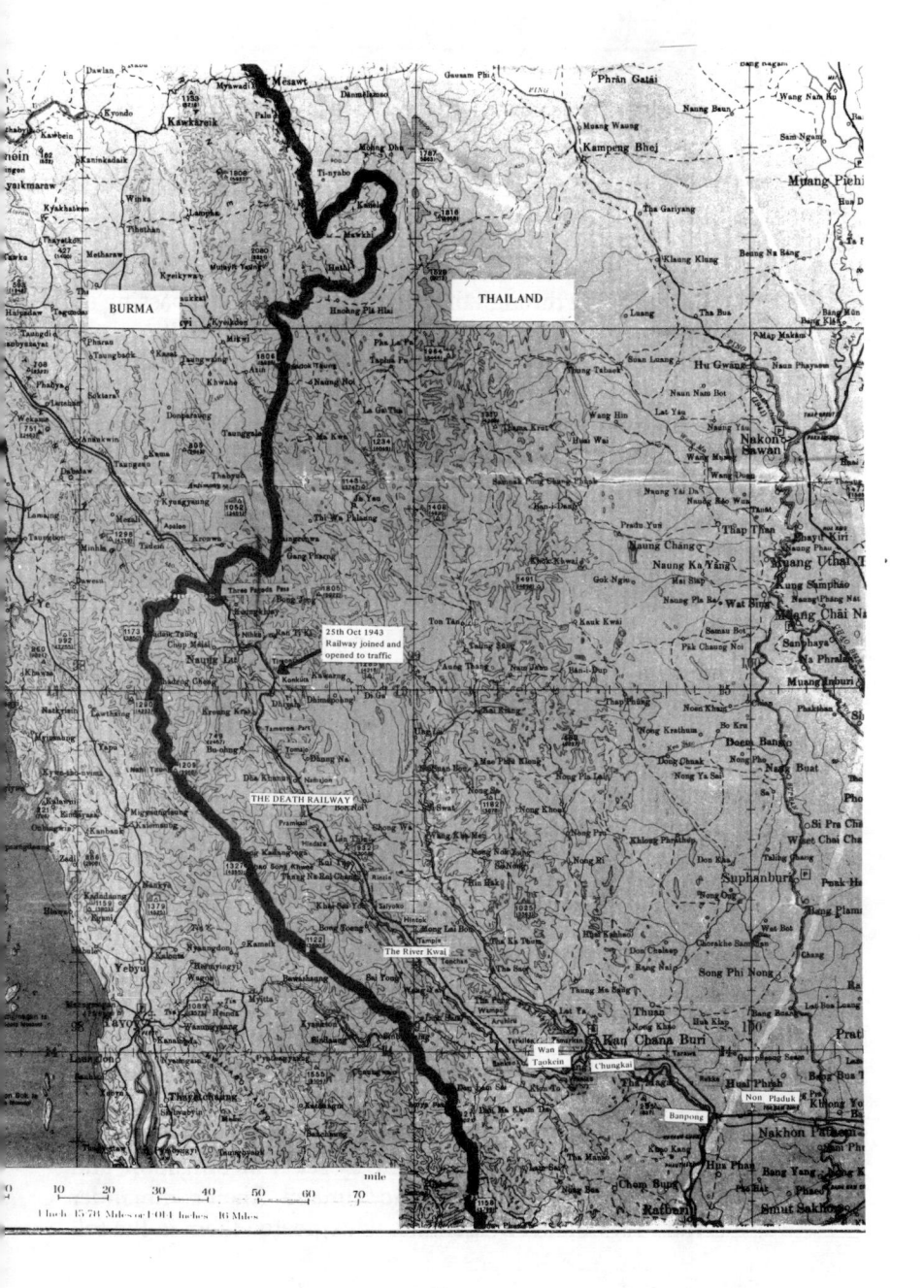

CHAPTER 8.

WUN LUN.

After trudging through the streets of Kanburi and passing its modern paper mill, a surprising building to find in a small country town, we assembled in a field on a river bank. It was our first acquaintance with the Kwae Noi, now known as the River Kwai. The rain continued unceasingly and how we all shivered, the sudden drop in temperature from the normal nineties Fahrenheit producing a chill factor.

With the water level running very high, we precariously crossed the three hundred yards or so to the opposite bank by barge. Bound for Wun Lun, a dozen miles along the Kwai, the first mile took us along a route through flat arable country. A guide led us on a slippery path dissecting padi fields and peanut cultivations but before long we plunged into forest, a dense area of jungle much as it had been at Tanjong Pau. After several miles of slipping and sliding through the dank undergrowth we came to a clearing where we halted for the night. We had arrived at a place called Chungkai, later destined to become a temporary community of some 10,000 souls, which was occupied by advance parties already working on the railway trace and having to finish erecting the familiar bamboo and atap huts in their spare time. The bulk of the subsequent 61,000 railway workforce arrived during the period October/November, with large numbers passing into the hinterland daily to join the six separate groups. Independently administered, 1, 2 and 3 operated from the Ban Pong end in Thailand and 3, 5 and 6 out of Thanbyuzayat in Burma. We found ourselves in No. 2 Group, whose headquarters had been set up at Chungkai under the command of Lt. Colonel Yanagida.

The majority of the Burmese workforce were Australian and Dutch who had been transported there by sea from Singapore and the Dutch East Indies, mainly Java and Sumatra. Their commander was a certain Lt. Colonel Magatomo, who greeted them in the following manner:-

> "It is a great pleasure to me to see you here at this place as I am Chief of War Prisoners in obedience to the Imperial Command issued by His Majesty the Emperor.
> The great Asiatic War has broken out due to the rising of Asians whose hearts were burnt with desire to live and preserve their Nations on account of the intrusion by British and Americans for the past many years. There is therefore no other reason for the Japanese to drive out the anti-Axis forces of arrogant and insolent British and American.
> It is not your fault but if your country does not wake up from its dream and discontinue their resistance ALL OF YOU WILL NOT BE RELEASED. However I will not treat you badly, for the sake of humanity, as you have no fighting power at all. The Imperial thoughts are inestimable and Imperial favours are infinite.
> I shall strictly manage all of you. Living, manners and deportment shall be according to the Nippon Army, because it is only possible to manage you, who are merely the remnants of a rabble army, by the orders of Military Regulations.
> In addition Nippon has great work for you to do building a railroad between Burma and Thailand of great interest to the World and you will have the honour to join in this great work."

Sobering words for his audience, many of whom indeed were destined 'not to be released'.

Conditions in Chungkai at this time were not good, the camp having recently suffered its annual flooding. As at Ban Pong, the latrines had flooded and the immediate areas were swamped with floating excreta. As usual we made the best of things and I went off to look to see if any of my friends happened to be among the inhabitants. To my delight I found Len Marshall in the first hut to be entered and he and his companions made room for me to sleep there, which was decidedly more comfortable than the open ground allocated to our party for the night. They also saw to it I received a more substantial meal than that provided for the 'passers through'. This was the first time Len and I had met since he had departed on a working party in Singapore some months earlier and we spent a very pleasant evening together.

After enjoying a good night's sleep for a change, we marched off the following morning, in the inevitable downpour, shortly after daybreak. Wun Lun was the next camp along the line about seven miles away, the route following the same type of muddy, slippery track. A mile or so before arrival the rain eased and, with the sun warming us up, I was able to take notice of the flora and fauna of the surrounding countryside. Sight of the camp though quickly brought me back down to earth.

First impressions indicated that we were bound for some sort of island. We halted on high ground at the end of a small peninsula, outside what was obviously the cook-house and another bamboo building that appeared to be a general store. Ordered to leave our kit on the ground - I was rather worried about this as my blanket was strapped around the outside of my haversack - we collected some bell tents and went down a steep path to the edge of the fast running, torrential river. Boarding a barge we crossed the short distance to the main area and clambered off over a mound along yet another slippery path until reaching the camp proper. We gazed across a muddy square of about an acre in size, which was a complete quagmire, at a few hastily assembled huts. Never had I seen such a morass.

Squelching through mud we were led to an area behind the huts, which seemed at one time to have been cropland cultivating tobacco. Like everything else was wherever we went, the ground was completely sodden and it was here that orders came to pitch the tents, utilizing some bamboo poles to provide a floor above the water line. It was night time before the task was completed and only then did we have our first meal, trudging back over the muddy square and over the water to collect it. We thought that now we could recover our kit but the Japanese said no, so we went back to the tents reflecting on our plight and wondering what sort of night lay ahead. Settling down on the bamboo I appeared to be protected from the water and, despite everything, I soon fell asleep until the early hours when the rains came once more. I awoke feeling damp and putting my hand down in the darkness found it submerged in the water that had risen to surround us. Not being able to do anything about it, we spent a dismal and fitful few hours remaining until the relief of morning; when it finally dawned - that night seemed to last forever - I was to be greeted with a very unpleasant shock.

Given access at last to our beleaguered kit, I found that mine had been tampered with. My only other shirt was missing and, more importantly, the full size heavy brown blanket, which was my main source of comfort, had also vanished. This big loss was to be continually felt over the next three years, both for warmth in the rainy seasons and coverage from the hordes of mosquitoes at all times. I was sure that the thief was one of our own kind, making it all the more depressing.

Located at the foot hills of the mountains, the nights at this time of the year were decidedly chilly and each morning we arose to heavy mists. The day time temperature hovered around 80°F, it was to reach the hundreds during the dry season, but now it plummeted in the early hours to around 45°F. Without the protection of a blanket I spent several miserable nights, literally shivering, until a newly acquired friend, Fred 'Taffy' Morgan, came to my rescue. We had met at Temple Hill, he was from 3rd Corps, and like me had joined the Territorial Army in 1939 and was in the Devon Regiment, having enlisted in Exeter where he was a student at St. Lukes teacher training college. Soon after my departure to Shanghai in 1939 he had left on a similar draft to join a regular battalion in India and had subsequently transferred to the Indian Army Corps of Clerks. It was only when, with the arrival of another party, we all vacated the tents and moved into one of the newly completed huts that he noticed my plight. His reaction was to generously invite me to share his own blanket, to his considerable discomfort.

Work started on the railway the day after our arrival. Assembling in the cold, misty early morning darkness on the muddy square, we had our first experience of the fatuous ritual of tenko *(roll-call)*. Each working group lined up five deep and the Korean guards counted the front rows and then multiplied by five, but unfortunately their arithmetic was weak. This often meant long periods of being kept standing whilst they argued over the count among themselves until a Jap N.C.O. would come along and sort things out. Finally everyone lined up at the Jap engineer's stores and collected the tools, spades with short handles and changkuls *(large, hoe type spades commonly used by coolies throughout Asia)*, after which we marched off to the railway trace. This had already been partly cleared and the Wun Lun force was responsible for a stretch of track about five miles long, linking up with parties operating from Chungkai in the south and Wan Yen to the north. Trekking two miles or so over very rough ground we arrived at the working area, which was covered with thick clumps of bamboo mostly fifteen to twenty feet high and several feet in diameter. The initial task was grubbing these out by brute force, gangs of men pulling on ropes tug-of war fashion to a chorus of ichi, ni, san, shi *(one, two, three, four)* from the directing Jap engineers.

As midday approached I was detailed to take several men back to camp to collect the lunch, which we carried back in kerosene cans. It was just cold, boiled rice and cold tea. After consumption of this welcome if unappetizing fare, work continued until five o'clock before returning to complete the routine of tenko, having been much delayed at the stores handing in our tools. The Korean there could not count either. Finally reaching our quarters, there was enough time to visit the river for a wash before darkness fell and then it was over to the cook-house for the evening meal of rice and stew. Afterwards groups sat around in the darkness in conversation until it was time to turn in at 'lights out' at 9.30 pm. Of course we had no lights to put out, it was just the army phrase for bedtime, other than occasional cigarette tins filled with coconut oil utilizing a piece of cord as a wick - basic but effective. So concluded our first day as railway builders.

Before long the track area was cleared of undergrowth and construction of the embankment began, earth having to be dug from the surrounding ground and then deposited on the trace to create a mound. Issued with baskets with a carrying capacity of just about a bushel, we operated in gangs of two; one digging and the other carrying. As the height of the embankment grew, it was to reach an eventual thirty feet, this system proved to be inefficient and more tiring so adjoining groups formed chains and passed the loaded baskets up the slope from hand to hand. The arrangement only operated on the whim of the Jap engineers in charge of the work and they quite often insisted on each man carrying his own basket. With the distance between the embankment and diggings naturally becoming further we next experimented by making stretchers from old rice sacks and bamboo poles. This method also did not always receive approval, sometimes being tolerated but more often resulting in verbal abuse and a few slaps to the face.

The Jap working period was of ten days duration and to start with we had the eleventh one off. This seemed fine until we became aware of their task work system whereby a given number of metres had to be completed in each period. Each period, regardless of any absences through sickness, the target was increased to proportions it was impossible to reach, so the days off became infrequent no matter how hard we toiled. There was nothing to do but accept our lot and be thankful that at least the rations, at this stage, had improved a little.

The main improvement was a variation from the daily 2 ounces of buffalo meat. Pork. Supplies of large, black pigs arrived by barge packed in crates and alive, although some had expired en route. The cooks soon slaughtered them and, after scrubbing the skins with hot water to remove the hairy coats, chopped them up for the cooking pot. An added bonus was the availability of pork fat, which was used to produce a reasonable version of a renown Malay dish of fried rice, pork and vegetables - Nasi Goring, which was everyone's favourite. Simultaneously, a more palatable vegetable, resembling a small lentil and about the size of a little pea, called Kachangijau made a welcome appearance. Finally, the rice ration had gone up to sixteen ounces per day, but as the sickness toll increased it was soon decreed that this was for workers only. The Japanese logic was that non-workers did not require so much energy, therefore they would only receive half-rations and we overcame this anomaly by lumping all rations together and distributing them equally.

The rates of pay were 15 cents a day for privates, 25 cents for sergeants and 40 cents warrant officers, so my wages for each of the ten day period as was 2.50 Ticals. At the time, there was to be rapid inflation within the year, the tical was valued at one shilling and twopence to the pound, so I was receiving under three shillings *(15p)* for my ten days of labour. A welfare fund was established to help in the purchase of eggs, peanuts and bananas for the sick and we all contributed one day's pay per period, thereby assisting as much as we could in providing vital vitamins needed for them to have any chance of recovery. Little as it was the money was very welcome, giving me the opportunity of buying a half blanket that someone had for sale. Well worn, bluish grey in colour and measuring just four feet by three, I gladly paid the required $1.50. It was hardly large enough and barely afforded coverage even when I curled myself up like a ball, but it would allow poor Taffy and I some undisturbed sleep.

Wun Lun even boasted a market. The local Thais had been allowed to set up stalls in a clearing between the camp and river, which we could visit during a one hour period each day upon returning from work. On offer, if one had the money, were a variety of extras such as duck eggs - hard boiled, fried or omelettes - and hands of bananas, banana fritters, peanuts and Red Bull cigarettes or cheroots. The fritters came served on banana leaves and were the favourite of many but I chose to limit my purchases to the more hygienic boiled eggs and bananas. The working pay did not go very far though and more people began to dispose of their valuables, for which it was necessary to insist in payment with prewar printed notes as the Thais did not like the inflationary currency being printed by the Japanese. The good notes were easily recognized, having been overprinted in red. The stall holders, mostly old hags, sat over charcoal fires cooking the various dishes on offer, their mouths always a deep red from incessant betel nut chewing. They also indulged in the constant spitting of the nut's red liquid, not very edifying to find in a food market.

There were exceptions, one being a voluptuous young girl known as Lulu who spoke some English. Not having set eyes on any females since capture, the lads naturally flocked to her stall and there were soon a number of rumours circulating about her. One such said that she was a British spy, which of course was romantic rubbish. Several fearsome looking Thais, wearing large curved knives in their belts, kept an eye on her and the other women to ensure that they were not cheated. They also kept away some amorous Koreans who showed a keen interest in Lulu's charms.

The sickness rate increased daily and there was some concern that within weeks of leaving Changi there was an outbreak of diphtheria. With only limited isolation facilities the disease spread quickly and it was saddening to see so many people with badly swollen throats, knowing that the doctors had little medicine to alleviate their suffering. Before long George Forsey died. His was to be the first death and it was a particular personal shock; I had known him since the Penang days, when he used to talk about his family at home in the Channel Islands and how he was worried about their fate under the German occupation. A few days later Sergeant Bell died of dysentery and then another colleague at Penang, Sergeant Jones, went down with a severe stomach disorder. He was evacuated back to Chungkai on the ration barge where slightly better facilities existed, but alas did not survive.

One of the hazards of grubbing out the huge bamboo clumps was getting scratched - just imagine cutting down huge rose bushes with thorns several inches long and you will have some idea of the problem. More often than not the result of the scratches, especially on the legs, would be an infection which soon turned into tropical ulcers and one morning Taffy awoke to find that he had one about the size of a five pence piece. The next day it turned into a horrible black colour, which indicated that the infection was diphthetic but, luckily for him, the doctors at this time still had sparse supplies of sulphonamide ointment that had been carefully husbanded since capture. The treatment worked and Taffy recovered after a week or so. As we had been sharing the same blanket, prior to purchasing my own, I was apprehensive regarding the scratches I had received but there were no developments.

The rainy season in Thailand is from May to November and as the weeks went by the wet conditions eased. The muddy square was now baked hard by the sun and efforts were continually being made to improve the environment. The open drains that had been dug were cleaned daily as an antimalarial measure and better, deeper latrines constructed in an endeavour to prevent further flooding. Fortunately we had with us a considerable number of officers, mostly from the Indian Army who had been separated from their sepoys when the latter were detained in Tanglin, and they had not yet been asked to work on the railway. They were of great help in doing this work in the camp, which spared us when we returned from our labours. The latrines were in the open and consisted of deep trenches some fifteen feet long by four feet wide, which were crossed by interspersed bamboos. One then duly squatted astride them, which was a hazardous operation in the dark of night time.

One morning the Japs ordered all of the officers to parade on the square. They assembled under the direction of the senior one, who happened to be my old C.O., Lt. Colonel Swinton, with whom I had recently become re-acquainted, and were told that they must work on the railway with the rest of us. The request was met with a flat refusal, with the colonel reminding the Japs that the terms of the Geneva Convention, which governed the rules of behaviour of belligerents to their captives, stipulated quite clearly that officer prisoners of war could not be made to work. So they stood their ground and an hour or two later, after a number of heated discussions, the Japs took positive action. Suddenly a truck came careering down the rough track that had now been cut along the line from Chungkai, full of armed Jap soldiers, which reversed into a position with the rear facing the ranks of officers. The covers opened and revealed a mounted machine gun crew in the firing position and it was announced that if the orders were not obeyed they would open fire at once. At this stage it was felt prudent to agree and negotiations ended with the formation of officer working battalions specializing in bridge building and the construction of culverts.

Whilst admiring the stand that had been made, we certainly needed their assistance. Since most of the initial camp work on the sanitation project had been completed, there had been some discontent among the other ranks with many feeling that the labours were not being fairly shared. This had particularly rankled when the Japs announced that all officers would be paid the equivalent of their opposite rank in the Japanese Army, whether working or not, although they had substantial deduction for what was termed 'board and lodging'. Even so most were left with about 30 Ticals every month, a small fortune to us, but each did make a contribution of 5 Ticals to the welfare fund.

At the end of November, nine months after capture, we were at long last given the opportunity to communicate with home when pre-printed cards were issued. They were very restricted, as can be seen from this example:-

"IMPERIAL JAPANESE ARMY

I am interned in ....

My health is excellent ....

I am ill in hospital ....

I am working for pay ....

I am not working ....

Please see that .... is taken care.

My love to you."

I entered the word Thailand on the first line, deleted the third and fifth, added my fiancee's name on the last and addressed it to my father. Being written with only a crude piece of pencil, it was not very legible but nevertheless survived to arrive safely at its destination fifteen months later in February 1944. Nominal rolls had been prepared by our Command HQ within the first few weeks in Changi and submitted to the Japs, who made no attempt whatsoever to notify the Red Cross. My card, therefore, was the first intimation that my family received that I was alive and a prisoner of war - albeit well out of date. This attitude of our captors was extremely cruel and caused our loved ones much heartache; I was to learn after the war that my poor mother had died in the summer of 1943 without ever learning of my fate. There had just been the official missing in action notification sent by Army Records in March 1942.

As late as April 1943 my father was to write:

"Ferndene,
Limes Road,
Egham, Surrey.

April 19th, 1943.

My dear Jack,
Once again a line to you which I hope will reach you and find you well. I have written several letters sent via the Red Cross and they have not been returned, but quite a lot of those that were sent to your last known address in Malaya have been.

Well, my dear boy, it is very difficult to write as I do not know where you are or anything about you, the last we heard from you was your letter dated January 12th 1942.

We can only hope that you are safe and well and some day we shall all be together again. That goes for all mothers sons in all countries.

I am pleased to say that Joan is OK but of course not very happy. If only we could get some news of you it would make a big difference to all of us.

This is spring once again, Jack, after one of the best winters I can remember. There was hardly any frost and the weather this week has been warm and sunny. Otherwise things are very quiet at Egham; Keeling, Saville and Beater from the Works have been called up but Wire, Hampstead and Parker are still here. Everyone asks about you and it is nice to know that you have plenty of friends around.

Well son, as I said before, it is a job to know how to write. This then is all and I trust to God this will reach you somewhere and then I shall be able to write a better letter.

Fond love from us all,
Kisses from Mum and
Your loving old Pop."

This letter did indeed reach me one year later in April 1944.

The daily walk to the trace, which became further away as the work progressed, in my only pair of socks and boots that were showing bad signs of wear and tear, had caused me to develop a blister on the right heel. It would not get better and eventually turned into an ulcer the size of a thumbnail so I had need to report to the medical officer, only to find that supplies of the vital sulphonamide had run out. He could only recommend the application of hot poultices for treatment, not an easy thing to arrange in our circumstances. It was at this time that I had the good fortune to meet Fred Rawley, a chirpy Cockney who had arrived in Singapore with the ill-fated 18th Division just ten days before the capitulation. Seeing my predicament, he told me to cut up what remained of my vest into strips to act as bandages and went off to light a fire over which they could be boiled. Twice a day he applied the poultices with considerable forcefulness and would not be denied. It worked and within a few weeks the wound had healed, although I carry the scar to this day.

A married man with a newly born child back home in Battersea, he had been conscripted in 1941 from his employment with Arding & Hobbs, the local department store. He was irrepressible, constantly helping people in need and always looking for ways to make some money; one example was the selling of ersatz coffee at 5 cents a cup. It was made from burned ground rice and soya beans, sweetened with gula malacca, and peddled around the huts at night in old kerosene cans to the cries of *"Hot, sweet and filthy"*.

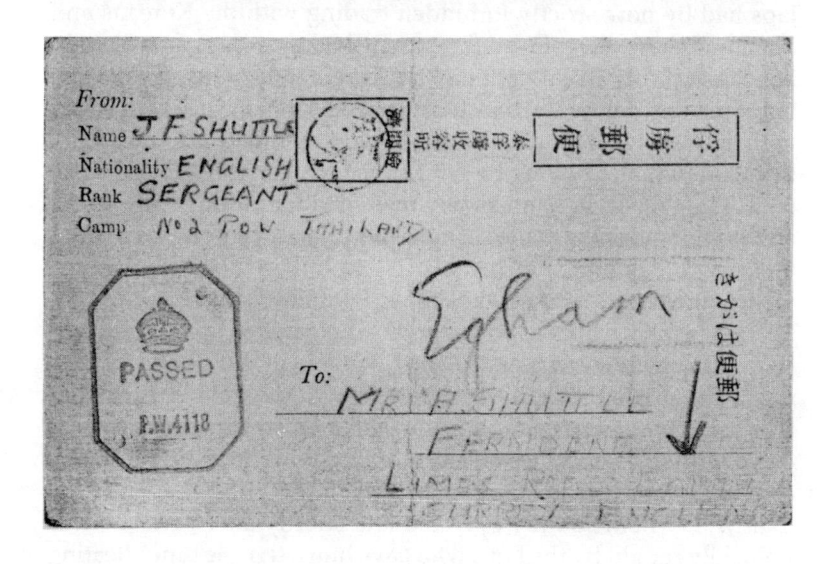

The first sparse communication that took so long to reach home. (Both sides shown).

'Mac' McKewan, a signalman who had come up with us from Changi and had been at Temple Hill, was another to benefit from Fred's kind hands. He became seriously ill with uraemia, a poisoned condition of excess urea in the blood, and the only hope for him was to extract as much liquid from his system as we possibly could. This entailed keeping his temperature high by wrapping him in hot blankets and Fred was at hand with a bonfire and kerosene cans, bullying people to loan their blankets. The next few critical days saw him constantly boiling the blankets and wrapping them around poor Mac. Once again the devoted attention paid off and he recovered, sadly only to succumb to cholera the following year.

Another interesting character among these same signalmen was one Sammy Nimco, also a Londoner from Tottenham in North London. Sammy soon became established as a contact man with the main camp racketeer. These people were natural entrepreneurs who had lost no time in setting up a buying and selling trade. The Japs had by now strictly forbidden trading with the Koreans and Thais and these men played the extremely dangerous game of making contact with the latter at nightly secret rendezvous. They were brave men and, although they took the risks for monetary gain, many of their deals were for altruistic reasons. Later their activities were to encompass the buying of extra supplies and drugs for the doctors. Still, they were handsomely rewarded for putting their 'necks on the line' and some made so much money that they offered a banking service, loaning sums against IOU's to be redeemed after the war. Utilizing the services of Sammy, I obtained satisfactory prices for two leather wallets and a combined cigarette case and lighter; such cases were very popular with smokers in the 1930s. Finally, not without some misgiving, I parted with the gold engagement ring that my fiancée had given me whilst on embarkation leave. I decided that I stood more chance of surviving to marry if it was converted into means of sustenance. Corporal Bluestone was the man with whom Sammy operated and shortly afterwards he was unluckily caught by the Japs, who gave him a terrible time. Beating him incessantly for hours on end, he was grilled to inform on the whole trading organization they suspected was in existence. It lasted two days, with strange rests between blows for coffee and biscuits - only the Japs could be so bizarre - but the corporal maintained his denial that anyone else was involved. Released, the doctors found that he had sustained a badly broken jaw which they somehow managed to wire up before sending him down to Chungkai. Our paths never crossed again.

With the approach of our first Christmas in captivity, we wondered if it would be any different to an ordinary working day. It was only after we had paraded for the routine tenko when the day arrived and had collected our tools, that it was announced that it would be treated as a yasumi *(rest)* day. Back we filed to return the unused tools and then departed to enjoy the luxury of nothing to do. We could visit the Thai market, which was open all day, or bathe leisurely in the river which had receded to almost fordable depth; completely different from the raging torrent we had witnessed earlier. Where we had crossed by barge a rope bridge straddled a small tributary twenty feet high, which had been submerged in the rainy season, and it was over this that the food orderlies trooped to collect our Christmas fayre. There had been some careful housekeeping for a period immediately beforehand and aided by purchases with a special donation from the welfare fund, the cooks gave us all a treat. Extra sugar came with the breakfast pap, whilst the usual rice only midday meal was enhanced with a small loaf made from ground rice and yeast extract spread with marmalade produced from tamarinds and limes. The latter was called a 'doover' derived, some said, from hors d'oeuvre whilst others said it was a 'do for later on'; this was due to the habit, when the delicacy was on the menu, of saving it until bedtime to fend off the hunger during the night. To return to the lunch, as I was in funds I bought myself two duck eggs and a share in a hand of bananas to add to it. In the evening, which was always the main meal, the stew contained quite liberal quantities of meat and was the thickest we had ever seen. The vegetables in it were pumpkin, marrow, Chinese radish, towgay bean shoots and kachanghijau which swamped the regulation half mess-tin full of rice. It was all followed by yet another 'doover' and I can honestly say that, for the first time, I felt satisfied at the end of a meal.

That night we kindled a bonfire and gathered around it for a singsong. Since leaving Changi there had been neither time nor any facilities for organized concerts but now some of the entertainers stepped forward with impromptu performances. A professional piano accordianist called Frankie had added to his burden on our strenuous journeys by carrying up his cumbersome instrument and he now provided the music. He was soon accompanied by our own

Lance Corporal Bradfield from the Surreys paying the cornet and then up stepped 'Capper' Parfitt, a diminutive sergeant from the Cambridgeshires, to sing. He bewitched us with his beautiful tenor voice with 'Because' and then led community singing of popular songs of the day. A padre then led us in a selection of Christmas Carols and concluded the gathering with prayers, after which we returned to our huts to retire at the regulation time of 9.30 pm. Seeing those silhouettes against the stark night sky in the glow of the flames from the fire, reverently singing carols on this our first Christmas in captivity, created an atmosphere that moved me deeply and in a strange way seemed to make my lot a little easier to bear. The next day it was back to embankment building, business as usual.

Although it was a working day, we were allowed another fireside sing along on New Year's Eve - the many Scots in camp having pressed for it. During one of the lulls between numbers, a voice from the back of the crowd suddenly cried out, *"Sing a bolero number, Johnny"*. Use of Johnny could only mean that the request had come from one of the Korean guards, it being their name for us, and the caller was in fact a guard already known as Y.M. Cagney. He had some knowledge of English and had already shown a willingness to fraternize, liking to talk about American films; his favourite film star was Jimmy Cagney and it was due to his mispronunciation of Jimmy that he received the nickname. His attitude was quite out of the ordinary, the behaviour of all the other guards being most antagonistic and requiring to be saluted at all times. Failure to do so would mean being summoned with the cry: *"Englisha soldierka, Buggairo Kurrah"* (fool, come here), followed by a blow to the head. Sometimes, depending on the guard's temper, the assault would be a clout with a rifle butt or the back edge of his bayonet. Occasionally the attacks were even more vicious, people receiving the rifle blow in the crotch and when they involuntarily bent over in pain were struck on the head with the bayonet.

At the conclusion of the singing, I made my way back to the huts reflecting 'Whither 1943?'. It was just as well that I could in no way imagine how awful that dreadful year would be.

One morning shortly afterwards I awoke with an abominable headache, experiencing severe pains at the back of my eyes. As the day progressed I felt bilious and could not face even the thought of food; by late afternoon I began to shiver violently and became aware of discomfort in the spleen. There was little doubt in my mind that I had fallen foul of malaria and my immediate companions, Fred and Taffy, loaned me their blankets to supplement my meagre one to try stopping the shivering. My temperature had risen alarmingly but the rigor continued uncontrollably, making all my limbs ache, for some hours before the fever subsided and left me soaked in perspiration. The next day I reported sick to Major Dunlop, a tall impressive Scottish doctor. He found that I had an enlarged spleen, which is a symptom of the disease, and took a blood slide that confirmed that it was positive BT malaria. Treatment was a seven day course of quinine pills *(still available in the early days, later we were provided with raw powder or none at all)*. The next day was fever free but it returned with a vengeance the following afternoon, the normal pattern of the complaint, but eased as the medicine worked. Now I was to learn of the unpleasant side effects of quinine when, at the end of the seven days, I was trembly and slightly deaf; not for the last time was I to contemplate whether the disease or the cure were more unpleasant.

Work on the embankment continued, but the metreage of the tasks set each ten days was reaching almost impossible proportions. Late in January a situation arose whereby much still remained uncompleted at the end of the statutory period so, at the end of that day, the work just carried on. Parties were sent back to camp to collect the evening meal and as night fell the surrounding undergrowth was set alight so that the toilers could see to work. The black silhouettes of the men against the bright red glowing background created a most sinister impression - Dante's Inferno come to life! By morning there was no respite as the required task had still not been completed, despite valiant efforts by the very weary workers. Relief finally came at 11 am when, after 27 hours continuous labour, orders were given to return to camp. Morale remained high and, I am proud to record, not a single man's spirit was broken by that mammoth work-shift; as the column approached the camp area everybody automatically formed into orderly ranks singing the soldiers bawdy lyrics of *"Colonel Bogey"* and the song, *"Sing as we go and let the world go by"*. This attitude did not go down very well with the guards or engineers and the Japanese gunzo *(sergeant)* in charge rushed about screaming abuse. With tempers high, tenko took over an hour, we were harangued and told to expect punishment. After much gesticulation and heated discussion, the gunzo selected ten men at random and marched them off to the guard house, where they were made to stand outside for the next twenty-four hours. This was a common form of treatment for offenders and the guards took sadistic pleasure in hitting them on the head each time patrols were changed. The ten were very unlucky but took it in good heart.

Until now I had sustained my smoking habit by purchasing the Red Bull cigarettes when I was in funds, but with rapid inflation they had become expensive and scarce. At 40 cents for a packet of ten, virtually three days pay, people were using the locally grown raw tobacco that had been cured by the Thais; groups of men shared in buying a kati *(1 $^1/_2$ lb)* and rolling it in whatever paper could be found. I tore out the pages of my Army Pay book and used them, but it was all rather foul and when I found that each 'draw' made me hiccup badly I decided it was time to stop. I was even more determined when I saw the horrible red liquid that poured forth from the tobacco when it was washed.

Soon there were more pressing matters to concern us when in the middle of February orders came to prepare to leave.

CHAPTER 9.

TARKILEN.

No one seemed to know our destination as we said goodbye to Wun Lun, our work having been completed in readiness for the advancing line laying gangs. Although life had not been pleasant there, we were soon to look back on it with envy recalling the market, tobacco plantation, kapok trees and peanut cultivation; we were never to see their like again. From time to time there had been illicit raids on the peanut crops, which improved the rations no end.

Marching north, we followed the railway trace through the secondary jungle along the embankment on which we had slaved over the past few months. Bypassing the next camp, Wun Yen, we finally arrived at Wan Taokien seven miles on and halted there for the night. It was virtually deserted, the former occupants also having moved on like ourselves, so at least we had some room. The climb up and down the embankment's thirty feet where, in this sector, the numerous bridges and culverts had not yet been completed, did not do my recently healed ulcer any good. When I removed my boots it was bleeding profusely but the faithful Fred soon bathed and bandaged the reopened wound, enabling me to be fit enough to continue the next morning.

Now we knew. The next stop was to be Tarkilen, twenty-three miles further on. Leaving in the early hours, at the halfway stage we came upon working parties from Bangkao camp; to my surprise one of them happened to be my old friend, Len, whom I had last seen when passing through Chungkai. On this occasion we were only able to call out our greetings as we passed each other by.

Tarkilen was a very small camp and seriously overcrowded, as we discovered to our cost upon our weary arrival. The few huts were built near the river and next to a Thai kampong, which boasted a wooden temple on stilts - a precaution against flooding. It was every man for himself and, finding no room whatsoever in any of the huts, a dozen of us claimed the ground space underneath the temple. Most of my companions here were sadly to die before the year was out, including Len Hay who as a Lance Corporal had been my section leader in Shanghai; the luckless Mac McKewan; the giant-sized Bill Prodger who was to lose his legs through tropical ulcers before his strength gave out and finally my good friend, Fred.

The stay in Tarkilen lasted three weeks and during this time there were no calls for railway working parties. It was all very strange, especially as the notorious 'speedo' period had already commenced up the line. One could only assume that the engineers had run into some problem or other and we welcomed the opportunity for our undernourished bodies to recover a little from the excesses we had been driven to over the previous months. The sojourn was not without incidents, though. When we had left Wun Lun the Japanese officers and N.C.O.s had already moved on, leaving command of the camp to Arri, a Korean 1st class private who had left us largely to our own devices. Now we were saddled with the hated Kokubu, a Japanese captain, and exposed to his drunken behaviour. His reputation had already spread along the line and even the Koreans were afraid of his unpredictability, one incurring his wrath within the first week here. The victim was 'Y.M. Cagney', still one of the guards and becoming more and more relaxed in our company.

He had pushed his luck too far. The Thai villagers were still living in the kampong, just forty feet across a lane opposite our temple, and although contact was expressly forbidden we were soon clandestinely trading with them. They always kept their distance but there were many delightful little brown children running about who acted as go-betweens. A lookout kept an eye for patrolling guards but there was nothing to worry about when 'Y.M.' was on duty, in fact he often volunteered to tip us off if anyone else was about. On some evenings he sat down among us in the dark, propping his rifle and bayonet against a post, and talked. His English had been learned, he said, on visits abroad as a member of the Korean Olympic swimming team. This may or may not have been true, but he was quite knowledgeable on popular songs and American films; one fellow had joined us who had retained a treasured guitar and 'Y.M.' was always requesting him to play various tunes. Obviously the blatant fraternization could not last.

He had not been seen for a day or so and then appeared dramatically. An escort party escorted him towards the river and then down the steep bank to the water's edge. Kokubu then arrived, accompanied by an orderly carrying a box which was placed on the ground for him to mount to reach 'Y.M.', who stood six feet tall. The offender was summoned forth and then received blow after blow from Kokubu's clenched fist, which went on until the striker tired. It was the last I saw of poor old 'Y.M.' and afterwards we had to be very careful, as from then on the other guards seemed even more vicious - especially Jungle Jim who was an ugly, fearsome creature.

After this incident we were banished from the temple and had to find space on the floor of one of the crowded huts. A few nights later our sleep was disturbed by the most unholy commotion, which turned out to be Kokubu well into his cups and charging about in a rage with drawn sword. Yelling at everyone to get up and assemble outside, he rushed into our hut very peeved because he felt we had not roused quickly enough for an immediate tenko. He was demented and even the Koreans had fled at the double and taken refuge outside the camp boundaries. The senior British officer, Lt. Colonel Milner, was summoned to stand to attention before the lunatic and, being a very correct officer of the old school, he delayed appearing until properly dressed. Kokubu immediately launched into the most violent assaults, continually knocking the colonel to the ground who each time regained his feet and stood rigidly to attention. It went on for at least fifteen minutes and was accepted with complete silence from the gallant victim; not once, either, was his Royal Indian Signal Corps bush hat dislodged. We had found a hero in this rather aloof and severe man.

Neither Fred nor I could settle down when Kokubu finally tired of his *'sport'*, so we went outside and sat on the river bank talking throughout the rest of the night. He told me about his youthful marriage and the arrival of the first child he had seen so little of; of the long connection the Rawley family had with the Arding & Hobbs store back home in Clapham Junction and of the many plans he had for the future. Little did I imagine as we talked that soon he would be no more.

When the time came to leave Tarkilen, my destination was to be Wampo South but he went on to Tarsao and upon departure was as full of spirit as ever. I was simply stunned when news reached me some months later that he had died from dysentery and, although only having known the man for a few months, I was deeply grieved;

even writing of the event all these years afterwards brings tears to my eyes. After my return home at the end of the war I was able, quite by chance, to bring some comfort to his family. In 1949 my wife and I were shopping to furnish our newly built house and visited the carpet department at Arding & Hobbs. As an assistant approached I received a considerable shock, for he was just like Fred and I felt I had to comment on the fact. It was indeed his younger brother, who was yet another Rawley following the family tradition, and it was gratifying to be able to express my appreciation of the kindnesses I had received. Until that coincidental meeting his family had never learned exactly what had happened to their lost son.

Our stay in Tarkilen continued to be eventful and I narrowly avoided becoming directly involved in another 'incident'. There being no official market facilities here, one of the Japs decided to indulge in a little private enterprise and established a stall on the river bank. He offered bananas, pomeloes, limes and tobacco that had been acquired at low prices from the Thais and as I walked by to bathe my companion stopped to buy a pomelo. Unfortunately making the mistake of haggling, as was the custom with the Thais back in Wun Lun, he was not served and instead received a beating. Additionally, his glasses were removed by the attacker and crunched on the ground prior to delivering the first punch to the jaw. I moved quickly on - it was not easy keeping out of trouble.

Next we had a domestic problem with Sammy Nimco. Whilst helping in the stores he espied some brown bottles labelled Scotts Emulsion, a well-known tonic. "Good," he thought to himself, "a quick swig will do me good," but the moment the liquid was swallowed he realized what a serious mistake he had made. The bottles were being used as containers for some potassium permanganate and poor Sammy rushed to the medics for assistance, who thrust salted water down him to induce vomiting. The prompt action worked, thankfully, and he was back to normal within a few days. It was a salutary experience.

Whilst on the subject of things doing one good, we noticed that iguanas roamed in this area and efforts at hunting them were made. We eventually caught one some three feet in length and when cooked the meat looked very similar to chicken; it had a definite earthy flavour and was much like the snake that we had already sampled.

Returning from a wood gathering party during the second week, it quickly became apparent that something serious was afoot. The camp teemed with heavily armed Japanese gendarmerie who were being formed into separate groups and dispatched to patrol the surrounding area. Four men had disappeared on an escape attempt.

For some time past Sergeants Kelly and Reay, together with Fusilier Timothy and Private Fitzgerald, had been preparing an escape plan. It entailed making for the coast at Maungmagan near Tavoy in Burma, some sixty miles from Tarkilen, following a route through dense mountainous unsurveyed jungle. When there a sea going boat would be commandeered to sail them the one thousand miles across the Bay of Bengal to India, the nearest friendly territory. It was a most formidable, almost impossible undertaking for undernourished Europeans in a mostly hostile Asian country. Having moved further up-country all four felt the time was right and approached the senior officer for permission; his reaction and that of his fellow officers was to explain the high risks involved and the enormity of their task. They were not to be dissuaded and the colonel gave his blessing, providing them with full support in the final preparations. Kelly, a member of the Royal Army Medical Corps, collected as many drugs and quinine as could be spared and they were all loaded with as many dry rations it was possible to carry. Given a special meal of steak, eggs, and sweet potato, gleaned by the Army Catering Corps sergeant-major in charge of the cook-house, the gallant four departed one evening on a specially constructed raft. Crossing the river, they quickly disappeared into the jungle and at tenko the absences were cleverly disguised by a previously organized flow of people making urgent visits to 'benjo'. The subterfuge lasted a couple of days, after which the colonel had to admit that four of his men were missing.

All of this was unknown to the majority and only came to light when the Japs began to act so frenziedly. In addition to their own troops, gangs of Thais joined in the search - large cash rewards having been rapidly promised - and reinforcements were arriving and moving into the jungle daily. On the tenth day the bid for freedom came to an end. Travelling only at night the four found the going in the dense jungle extremely tough, having had to hack their way through the undergrowth yard by yard for most of the time. With the hordes after them, even restriction to the hours of darkness proved to be of insufficient protection and they were caught near the Burmese border, just sixteen miles away.

Private Fitzgerald was shot dead resisting arrest and the remaining three were marched back to camp, with their wrists lashed together, whereupon the brave men were made to stand outside the guardroom. No food was provided, all access was forbidden, and there they remained until leaving for Banpong early the next morning. They then appeared at a so called trial and were immediately sentenced to death by firing squad. The executions took place within a few days.

Only six weeks previously a similar atrocity occurred, this time at Chungkai, involving four private soldiers from my old 'B' Company of the East Surreys. Cleaver, Croker and Richardson were regular soldiers, firm friends and in the same mould as Harry 'Shag' Waters - another East Surrey who had met the same fate back at Changi during the Selarang incident. Dorval was a French Canadian who had enlisted in 1940 during our stay in Shanghai. I knew the first three very well and was aggrieved to learn later of their failed escape attempt from Tamarkan and subsequent murders.

As the Chungkai cemetery sadly grew, many requests were made in the following years for their remains to be transferred but to no avail. The graves however were not neglected. A year later I passed them by when out on a bamboo collecting chore and was pleased to observe that the local Thais had built a mound of rocks around them, which were kept adorned with fresh flowers. Both groups of these gallant gentlemen are now interred in the beautiful War Graves Commission Cemetery at Kanchanaburi.

The man who ordered these executions, Major General Sasa Akiro, was tried in 1946 for these crimes, found guilty and hanged.

Later in that eventful year, July 1943, another escape was attempted, this time from Sonkurai some 125 miles further up the line. A larger group, consisting of eight British officers and one corporal together with an Indian seaman, they made for Ye on the Burmese coast about sixty miles away. After six undetected weeks some of the party arrived, but the appalling task of negotiating the terrible terrain of the jungle-clad Taungnyo mountain range had taken its toll. Five of them had died en route. The remainder were barely alive themselves when they struggled into Karni, where they were given succour by the villagers and grateful at being so befriended. Unfortunately the Headman of Karni got wind of the handsome reward for escaped prisoners and betrayed them to the Japs. For the whole of the next year the five were constantly threatened with execution, but after being sent back to Singapore actually received the courtesy of a trial in June 1944. A sentence was passed committing them to 10 years in Outram Road prison, where they were serving when release came in August 1945.

One evening at 6 pm early in April orders came suddenly to pack and leave camp immediately, whereupon we marched off to the railway line which by now was operating up to a place called Aruhiro. Destination unknown, I was nevertheless pleased to be moving on. Tarkilen had been a poor sort of place and whilst there I developed ringworm on both legs, which were now beginning to turn septic. Additionally, early signs of small ulcers had appeared on my ankles and the lower side of both legs.

CHAPTER 10.

WAMPO SOUTH.

It was twelve midnight before a lumbering old wood burning locomotive hove into sight. Filling the flat, open trucks of the train we chugged slowly along up the continuously rising gradient over a distance of about ten miles to the end of the track so far completed. The short journey was not without some foreboding; would there be any subsidence, we wondered, bearing in mind our earlier attempts at sabotage by burying the occasional rotting tree when building the embankment! Although very rickety we arrived all in one piece at Aruhira, already rechristened Arrowhill by the lads. It was difficult in the black night air to see much, but there were indications that some sort of marshalling yards had been built here. The area was even more mountainous but, after marching in a steady climb for about four miles, we suddenly descended and arrived at what seemed to be a gravelly beach. A halt was called and then we learned that this was where we would be staying for the rest of the night, so I scooped out several handfuls of pebbles to accommodate my hips and settled down to sleep through the remaining hours before sunrise. When daylight dawned we found that the 'beach' was actually part of a dried up river basin and above, about one hundred yards away, were towering cliffs of solid rock rising above a sharp bend in the river. This was Wampo South, the first of a trio of camps - the others being Central and North - established for one of the most perilous and difficult projects on the whole line.

The cliff, which projected out over the river, was a major obstacle to the direction of the line and we were to join in the task of blasting the rock away from the top to create a ledge. A viaduct would then have to be built close in to the face, taking the track around the sharp bend for a distance of a quarter a mile. It was a colossal job and, as we had moved into the camp that day and saw the thousands of men already at work completing the embankment that ran up to the proposed viaduct, I could scarcely believe my eyes. There were so many of them, just like a colony of ants as they toiled away silhouetted against the skyline. The actual height would be seventy-five feet from the river bed and the supports made from green timbers cut down in the surrounding jungle, all to be erected without the aid of any mechanical equipment, just us and a few elephants. Work had just started on construction of the concrete base and blasting the rock on the cliff; the little men told us that the project had to be completed within three weeks, which everyone thought was impossible.

The main body of workers were housed in the other two camps, but we had been directed to a handful of very poor huts virtually on the work site. Twelve men squeezed into bays ten feet wide and five deep and everybody started work immediately, some going up on the rock face and the others to a wood yard. We returned in the evening to find all of the bed spaces occupied bv those employed on the night shift, with whom the accommodation had to be shared.

High up on the cliff, pairs of men drilled holes one metre deep, one wielding a sledge hammer whilst his mate held the steel drill. It was hard work breaking through the granite and went on all day until, each evening, the engineers filled in holes with sticks of dynamite in preparation to blasting. This took place at 6.30pm and was heralded by the raising of a red flag plus the sounding of a warning bugle; debris fell all over the camp and we had to take cover as best we could in the surrounding jungle. This heralded the departure of the night workers, who now climbed the mountainside and, under the glare of kerosene lanterns suspended from above, cleared away the loose material and prepared the ledge for the next day's operations.

On our side of the river there was great activity at the wood yard. Felled tree trunks arrived by bullock cart from lumber gangs in the jungle and were then cut to length and shape, prior to being sent across the river for erection as the main viaduct supports. I found myself with a partner on a large cross cut saw and we sawed away continuously on the huge lumps of timber which measured about a metre in diameter. As our pace slowed later in the hot, humid day we came in for much verbal abuse from our overseers who sometimes pulled one of the team away, sawed furiously and yelled out that Nippon were No. 1 and we were No. 10. After a few minutes we would be back and he resumed lolling in the sun!

When the timbers were ready three elephants dragged them on a sled to the edge of the river, from where they floated across to the site for erection. Another of their jobs was lifting and stacking accumulated stocks, the great gentle creatures delicately stepping between the rows of wood with ease. At night their mahouts securely chained each one to a stout tree, especially before blasting took place - they did not like this at all and bellowed loudly. Afterwards they were fed on the beach from large ration baskets full to the brim and then taken into the water to bathe, submerging their whole frame with just the top of the head protruding through the surface.

I suppose the most hazardous work of all was the actual erection. With the main green timber supports wedged into position, cross piece supports, which were made from splitting saplings down the middle, had to be affixed with iron staples some nine inches long. This entailed perilous climbs on the flimsy structure up to seventy-five feet high to drive them into position, but it did not prevent the irate engineers striking blows up there if things were not proceeding to their liking. As the construction progressed it became quite obvious that there would be no platform on the top, just sleepers laid across from side to side to take the rails. Upon completion we walked over it, stepping from sleeper to sleeper; there

Wampo viaduct after completion.

was nothing in between to prevent a drop to the water far below.

By the end of the first week on the crosscut my hands were red raw from blisters so I was relieved one morning to be detailed to join a sapling gathering party. The rains started early that year and on this particular day it was simply teeming when we set off with a Jap NCO in charge, who was wearing one of their cheap regulation raincoats which dragged around his heels. Soon drenched by the wet undergrowth we plodded on some miles until finding a selection of young trees to fell and, despite the appalling weather, found the task more to our liking than the wood-yard sawing. Furthermore, on breaking at midday to eat our cold rice, the NCO acted in a friendly manner and actually handed round some cigarettes. Returning in the evening he lost the way in the bush but we made it back in time for our meal, though only owing to one of the lads climbing a large tree to establish our bearings. Before we dismissed, he noticed my blistered, bleeding hands and took me to the Jap's own first aid tent, a precaution for possible blasting injuries, took some iodine from a shelf and indicated that I apply some. Apart from 'Y.M.', this was the only time before or after that anyone showed any consideration to our plight.

Despite the heavy rain experienced that day, the rainy season was only in the early stages. In the wake of the south west monsoons, that would bring the torrential rains to cause the annual flooding, the temperature had risen over the hundred degrees Fahrenheit mark. The result was heavy electric storms, usually breaking out in late afternoon, producing incredibly loud claps of thunder which reverberated between the hills lining the valley. Sometimes the storms occurred at night and it was in the aftermath of one that our sapling gathering party had gone out.

The change of season brought an invasion of butterflies. The very first time they were seen was early in the morning, when huge clouds came flying in the same direction down through the valley. Suddenly they were everywhere as large numbers appeared - name a colour and it was there. Greens of many shades; blues; sepia and other browns; lemon; white; orange and finally copper, all varying between the plain, striped and other exotic patterns. Budding lepidopterists among us were excited by the phenomenon but the rest found that the sheer numbers caused them to be a pest, beauty or no. Consequently it was with some relief when they disappeared suddenly as soon as the next thunderstorm broke out. It was not the end, though, because they returned with a vengeance the next sunny morning and we had to suffer their presence for several more days. Only then did they leave us in peace and everyone could again eat without disturbance. I could cope with the flies but this had been ridiculous.

One night we saw great long columns of men passing along the high cliffs on the other side of the river. No contact could be made and we had no idea who they were, but later learned that they comprised the ill-fated 'F' Force; reinforcements on their way up from Changi. Tokyo had decreed that the railway must be completed by October 1943 but, with so many of the original workers falling sick with malnutrition related diseases, we were behind schedule. Accordingly, another 7,000 men were demanded by the engineers from those prisoners still remaining in Singapore, so 'F' Force were despatched. They came from some 16,000 there, many of them patients in Roberts Hospital or former ones on the way to recovery. All blissfully unaware of what was happening in Thailand they were told, as we had been, that the move was to be to a better equipped camp with access to improved food supplies. It was even suggested that the sick should be included and room was indeed found on one of the trains for a piano but this was never seen again. The misrepresentation was despicable. Singapore Command planned to build an airport at Changi using these men, so they only agreed to send them on the understanding that the force returned upon completion of the railway.

So they came and met with a hostile reception. No assistance was afforded when the trains arrived at Ban Pong and they were made to march all the way up the line to Sonkurai, a distance of 190 miles. This was near to Three Pagoda Pass where the track crossed into Burma; it took them six days and nights. Coming immediately after that dreadful five day train journey from Singapore, the trek took a heavy toll and many fell by the wayside with dysentery and malaria as well as pure exhaustion. When we saw them at Wampo they had already covered seventy miles on foot, even though the railway was now operative from Ban Pong to the now nearly finished viaduct. The working camps in the Sonkurai area that housed them were absolutely appalling and the arrival coincided with the relentless 'speedo' period. Even more hands were demanded and they were joined in early May by the 2,500 strong 'H' Force, a mixture of British, Australians and Dutch. It was at this time that a cholera epidemic broke out and, although prevalent everywhere, the newcomers were particularly badly hit. By the time the railway was completed in October 1943, 1700 had lost their lives and only 7,800 survived the six months to return to Changi. The lucky ones who had stayed there were horrified at the deterioration in their condition and incredulously learned for the first time how things were for us.

By mid April the viaduct was ready for the rails to be placed in position. They had said three weeks and three weeks it was; nobody but the Japs could have driven underfed, ill-equipped and badly accommodated workers with such ferocity to achieve their aims. Within a few more days the first train cautiously crawled across and fifty years on modern trains continue to do so daily. There are still eighty miles of the railway from Ban Pong in commercial use but the remainder has long since been reclaimed by the jungle.

The job finished, it was time to leave for Takunun fifty miles further up north but I did not go on. Major Dunlop was concerned with my physical condition, which by now was quite poor. My hands had not improved, the ringworm had turned septic and the ulcers were getting bigger; in addition I was now painfully thin, so much so that my heartbeat was clearly visible, just like the pendulum of a clock. He therefore detailed me to take a small party of other sick back to Chungkai. Everybody was pleased to be leaving, whether it was up country or down, because surely the food could not be worse wherever one went. Here we existed on rice and onion water, plus some dehydrated vegetable and the occasional dried stinkfish.

Bidding farewell to my comrades in adversity, I set off walking perilously over the viaduct and down the line the few miles to Arrowhill to await a train.

CHAPTER 11.

BACK TO CHUNGKAI.

Efficient movement control not being one of the Japanese talents, we experienced the usual long wait but eventually a train lumbered along for us to clamber aboard the flat open wagons. After various stops at halts near the old working camps, we finally lurched to a jerky stop after passing through a narrow cutting outside our destination. Alighting from the train I thought how fortunate I was not to have been on that long trek north with 'F' and 'H' Forces.

The camp entrance was about one mile along a dirt road, built since we were last here, and upon arrival there was the inevitable search. Such searches took place at all times when moving, before and again after entering a new camp. At last passing into the camp after the guards had finished arguing over the tenko numbers *(there were only two dozen of us but they still had difficulty in getting it right)*, we were allocated a hut near the entrance.

Chungkai had changed quite markedly in the six months since the previous November. There was a much larger guardhouse standing near a tall lookout tower and opposite were several huts housing the Jap administration offices. The former Thai village had disappeared, they had been banished, and a bamboo stockade had been erected around the perimeter. Many more huts had gone up, with the old original ones now acting as a hospital area. Finally, Yanagida had established 2 Group Headquarters here.

Our hut turned out to be in a very dilapidated state, it having been one of the first to be built by inexperienced hands. There was a storm that night, when we found to our discomfort just how bad it was. There were great gaps in the roof and the rain simply gushed through it, churning up the ground between the sleeping platforms. Even more depressing was the infestation, the bamboo slats being absolutely alive with bed bugs and body lice; to get any sleep at all we decided to spend the dry nights lying on the ground outside. Only the persistent mosquitoes would bother us here, we thought,

Hut construction at Chungkai, 1943.

but sometimes the Korean guards objected and ran about kicking and shouting loudly to get back inside.

To my pleasure I discovered that Len was here. When the Chungkai sector was complete he had bypassed us at Wun Lun and gone up to Bangkau, where he had a bad bout of dysentery. By the time of my arrival he was recovering but still subject to attacks of colitis. Despite the overcrowding room was found for me in his bay, alongside Leo Lavender, John Huskisson, 'Holly' Hollyman and Chris Repton. Leo was a nice little London Jew formerly employed in the tea trade; John was also a Londoner and worked in a bank; Holly had been one of our original nineteen members of 2nd Echelon - I never met any of the rest again - and finally Chris, who had come to Malaya with 3rd Corps HQ. He was a tall, fair lad from Chertsey in Surrey whose father was in the film industry.

First priority was to attend the skin clinic that had been established, where I quickly received daily treatment of sulphonamide, which was still available in limited quantities. Told to keep the budding ulcers covered up I tore up the remainder of my last vest into narrow strips for bandages, applying them in the same manner as poor Fred had done for me earlier. With regular attention both the ulcers and the ringworm eventually healed, leaving smooth areas on both legs - a permanent reminder.

I soon learned that a number of the inhabitants were suffering from scabies, Leo in particular being badly infected. He used to drive us all mad by continuously rubbing his hands on the rough bamboo slats in an endeavour to relieve the awful irritation. This unpleasant scourge had broken out due to the overcrowded, insanitary conditions encouraging the breeding of lice and was the result of constant biting by these bloated, loathsome pests. Attacking the tenderest parts of the anatomy, the scabies parasite burrows under the skin to lay its eggs, which causes the terrible irritation, creating suppurations varying in length from an eighth to a quarter of an inch. Without rapid treatment these soon turn septic, adding painful throbbing to the discomfort of the irritation. The worst affected areas were between the fingers, the base of the palm, stomach and the most tormenting of all, the genitals. It was not long before I too was infected.

So rife was the pestilence that, even though a special decontamination unit was established, there was a minimum waiting period of 14 days for treatment. This entailed enduring a distressing fortnight but during the wait I did my best to keep things under control. Borrowing a hard bristle hair brush I scrubbed the sores open in the river, which tended to ease the irritation and check the development of the poisoning. When my turn arrived I reported to the anti-scabies unit, which was located on the river bank halfway between the cook-house and ablution sections. It was a two day course and one had to bring half of one's meagre clothing each day for boiling in the two large containers, which were stoked by open fires. Queuing completely naked we were scrubbed all over by volunteer medical orderlies, to open up all of the sores, and then painted with a shaving brush dipped in a sulphur paste. This sticky yellow concoction had a coconut oil base and the application caused very painful smarting, thus everybody ran up and down the river bank until it eased. It was in fact quite hilarious. The same procedure occurred on the second day and the treatment worked very satisfactorily, clearing it up immediately. Unfortunately, I became infected again some months later, so had to go through the misery once more.

Now a base camp, people were continually on the move as some of the sick recovered sufficiently to go back up the line. By far the larger movements though were the ever increasing parties arriving, many bringing quite seriously ill men. Ten of the 200 feet long huts had been designated the hospital area and they were soon full to overflowing; it was not long before the death rate grew alarmingly. It had already become necessary to establish a cemetery and this had been located on the eastern perimeter, actually a most beautiful setting surrounded by large trees, gorgeous hibiscus hedges and rows of zinnias, cannas and other shrubs and bushes. A large wooden cross was made and erected in the most prominent part of this sad place where, by the time we left, there would be over 1200 graves. After the war, the War Graves Commission located as many bodies as possible along the railway route and re-buried the remains at Chungkai and Kanchanaburi in Thailand and Thanbyuzayat in Burma, the numbers resting there being 1740, 6982 and 3771 respectively. Our wooden cross has now been replaced by a magnificent one of stone which proudly stands on the original site. Every grave has a granite plinth, faced with a bronze plate giving full particulars of the man interred therein and the whole area is laid out in rows of neat grass paths. The same trees, flowers and bushes still adorn it and regular maintenance is reverently provided by full time

Chungkai Cemetery in 1944.

Below: As it was when re-visited in 1960.

Bottom: The memorial erected there by the War Graves Commission.

The River Kwai at Chungkai.

This was the terrain which we dug to build embankment.

The cookhouse at Chungkai.

*A hut interior.
Note the reader's clompers.*

Two views of camp life in Chungkai.

attendants. The camp area is now covered with secondary jungle and the cemetery stands in splendid isolation near the river bank. At its entrance a stone monument lists all of the names of the fallen and is inscribed;

"IN HONOURED REMEMBRANCE OF THE FORTITUDE AND SACRIFICE OF THAT VALIANT COMPANY WHO PERISHED WHILST BUILDING THE RAILWAY FROM THAILAND TO BURMA DURING THEIR LONG CAPTIVITY. THOSE WHO HAVE NO KNOWN GRAVE ARE COMMEMORATED BY NAME AT RANGOON, SINGAPORE AND HONG KONG AND THEIR COMRADES REST IN THE THREE CEMETERIES OF KANCHANABURI, CHUNGKAI AND THANBYZAYAT. **I WILL MAKE YOU A NAME AND A PRAISE AMONG THE PEOPLE OF THE EARTH WHEN TURN I BACK YOUR CAPTIVITY BEFORE YOUR EYES SAITH THE LORD"**

Towards the end of 1943, when Chungkai had grown into a community of 10,000 British, Australian and Dutch, as many as eighteen burials were taking place a day. There were two funeral processions, one in the morning and another at evening time, the bodies sewn into rice sacks and borne by orderlies on stretchers. Comrades of the dead attended, dressed as smartly as possible, and a bugler was always on hand to play the last post. When we heard the call the whole camp halted and stood to attention.

Bill Panniers died in May. He was a young bank clerk from Walthamstow in North London serving in the Royal Signals as a sergeant and we had first met at Wun Lun. In discussing food in general and torturing ourselves in contemplating exotic dishes, he mentioned visiting the home of a young lady when stationed at Egham. Prior to leaving with the 18th Division in 1941 he had become engaged to be married to her and proudly showed me some photographs. She was in fact Doreen Macey, the sister of an old school friend, and from then on Bill never stopped talking to me about her.

A few weeks after arriving at Wun Lun he developed a nasty boil in one of his armpits, which was most persistent despite being lanced and bathed daily, and was sent down to Chungkai. Looking him up when I arrived there six months later I found him in the hospital section in a serious condition, suffering from wet beriberi. This ghastly complaint had by now become very common, the direct result of a diet of watery rice and a deficiency of the vital B2 vitamin. Early symptoms are the swelling of feet and legs, unresponsive reflexes and indentation when pressing the flesh adjacent to the shin bone. Untreated, the adoema advances to huge proportions; the legs becoming trunk-like; the stomach as large as a pregnant woman; the testicles the size of footballs and the face as free of wrinkles as a baby. Eventually, with the high level of water in the system reaching the heart, death results from cardiac failure. The only salvation was special diet from the inadequate resources, which sometimes effected recovery, sometimes not. Poor Bill was a lost cause and within one month the end came. I pledged myself to tell Doreen of the tragic event when, I hoped, I had survived. Upon finally returning home I learned that her family had already been told of his sad loss, but I did not see her personally due to her absence in Canada. In the intervening period she had met a Canadian Serviceman, married and become a mother. So I never carried out my promise. In mitigation I suppose that she did not place as much seriousness to the liaison as perhaps Bill had - it was a short wartime romance - and he had, like myself, been posted missing.

    Constant perspiration in the tropical humidity took its toll on my few remaining clothes, the one pair of shorts becoming virtual rags with only the waistband and crotch still intact. The khaki drill slacks wore through at both knees and the seat, but I was able to effect some repairs by sewing on patches using some blue material that I had managed to scrounge. They gave the appearance of a patchwork quilt but it was practical, which was just as well because at no time were we issued with any clothing or footwear.

    The problem of shodding our feet was solved with 'clompers', a form of footwear commonly worn by Asiatics. Fortunately there were plenty of kapok trees in the area to provide the lightweight wood from which they could be roughly shaped. Nailing pieces of rubber, cut from old tyres, across the front end to accommodate the toes we obtained perfectly comfortable and effective footwear. Such types of shoe are now quite fashionable everywhere with young ladies and I am taken back to those days every summer when I see girls tripping along, clonk, clonk. It was amazing how quickly we adapted to them, being able to run and play games with ease. They were especially welcome to me, because for a long time the ulcer on my heel made it impossible to wear what was left of my boots. So, when a Dutchman expressed an interest in them I went to see him. His party, who had recently arrived from Burma, were quartered on the far side of the camp where I soon found him. His proposition entailed a straight exchange for a pair of green Dutch army shorts, which were in nearly new condition and I quickly did a deal. After being dressed in tatters for such a long period, being able to wear such smart shorts did wonders to my morale and saved me from having to resort to using a 'Jap-Happy' *(a sort of loincloth)*. It was one way of solving the ever present clothing problem, usually made from a piece of material about ten inches wide and twenty-four inches long. The garment was copied from the Japs and Koreans, who wore a similar item when off duty or bathing - hence its name. The tag was also given to men who accepted jobs in the Japanese kitchens, tempted by the possibility of extra food.

Since joining the sick I no longer received any pay and, having sold the last of my valuables, now had no money at all so was having to manage on the standard rations. There was a canteen of sorts, run by Thais under Jap control, situated between our hut and the hospital section. We could see it quite clearly and watched with envy as the customers, mostly officers who were the only ones in funds, called there and purchased Mah Mee *(a kind of fried noodle)*, eggs, bananas and ersatz coffee. The reign of the 'hot, sweet and filthy' pedlars had passed.

The river was our lifeline. Supplies were delivered by barge to the stores adjacent to the cook-house, which was situated at the northern end of the camp where the river turned sharply. Ablutions took place down stream round the bend, where we cleansed ourselves by bathing whenever the opportunity arose, although soap was always in short supply. On the rare occasions when any was issued it was of very poor quality, mainly made from soda, being hard and with blue veins running through the centre; the high soda content also made it sweat and quickly evaporate. To some extent I solved the problem by scrubbing my clothing with grit from the river bed, which proved to be a fair substitute. Facilities for dental hygiene were minimal, toothpaste being nonexistent and toothbrushes irreplaceable. The bristles on mine lasted for the first year and whilst it lasted I brushed my teeth vigorously daily, saving a little tea to ensure not having to use unboiled water. When the bristles finally gave out I turned to charcoal, made from burnt wood on the cook-house fires; it was better than nothing

With the continued shortage of soap, shaving was restricted to twice weekly. Official camp barbers were appointed and every Monday and Friday I presented myself to one of the long queues and, upon reaching its head, lathered up in cold water with a communal shaving brush. The volunteer barbers, mainly professionals in civilian life, used 'cut-throat' razors and when they finished each shave wiped the lather off on banana leaves. Sometimes, if I could scrounge the soap, George Greaves gave me extra shaves using his ordinary stainless steel table knife. He kept this sharpened by regular honing on a barber friend's carbon stone and it proved very effective. George, who was a Lance Corporal in the Cambridgeshires, made a very good job and at the same time kept my pencil slim moustache in good trim, which made me feel less scruffy. The battle to keep presentable in appearance was constant, and to help I nipped down to the river early each morning and collected a haversack full of water. I was then able to have a wash of sorts at the start of the day, rather than waiting for the official bathing period late in the afternoon. The still water doubled as a mirror, clear enough to be used to comb my hair. It made me feel a lot better.

As the weeks went by Len and I began to improve in health and were able to join the few paid workers employed locally, which for a while provided some very welcome money. He went into the cook-house and I was sent to some gardens that the Japs had established for themselves just outside the camp boundary. The work was mainly weeding, up and down the rows on our knees, and although irksome was by far preferable to the railway slaving up country. An alternative chore was operating the Jap water filtering plant. This was a simple system consisting of a five cubic feet tank, which we kept filled from the river by forming a human chain up the river bank. Teams of two then manned a pump to drive the filtered water through a chute into another 'clean' tank, which then had to be manhandled to the Japanese quarters.

Our diet remained little changed. It was 'pap' rice for breakfast, half a mess-tin of plain boiled rice at midday and the same, plus jungle stew, in the evening. The meat *(buffalo)* ration was two ounces per man per day, delivered on hoof which the cook-house staff had to slaughter. Len's employment there was a definite bonus, enabling him to obtain larger helpings, a staff perk that no one begrudged the hard-working cooks. He was able to bring us the occasional luxury, either a little beef tea or perhaps some tripe. We avidly devoured the latter, despite its foul smell.

At last we were able to move out of our poor infested hut, settling into a fresh, but still old, one at the bottom of the southern end of the camp next to the hospital section. With more and more people coming back from the line, the camp expanded rapidly. New huts went up in row upon row all along the mile stretch from the camp offices to the railway, whilst the original dilapidated ones we had occupied were pulled down and replaced. The change of accommodation, though, did not stop us from regular soakings now that the monsoon period was approaching its zenith.

As the month of June passed there continued the violent thunderstorms. Every afternoon at four o'clock the skies darkened to an almost night like density and the usual tremendous ones broke out about us. The thunder and lightning were of frightening severity but the heavy monsoon rainfall had its advantages, providing a natural shower bath. We stripped off delightedly to wallow in the fresh water as it pelted down, even though there was little that could be done to prevent having to troop back inside with muddy bare feet.

When our captors first decided to establish a base camp here, they were warned by the local Thais that the area was notorious for severe flooding yearly. Located in a delta between two major rivers, the Mae Klong and the Kwae Noi *(Kwai)*, which converged at Kanchanaburi further down stream, it was vulnerable from two different sources. The heavy continuous rain along the whole course of the rivers had turned them into raging torrents and eventually the banks burst and swamped Chungkai, the flood coming directly from the Kwai and, at our rear, from the overflowing Mae Klong. My block of huts were situated in the lowest area and were the first to be affected. It all happened very quickly, when on one morning we awoke to find the floor seeping with water; by late in the afternoon it was over one foot deep. As we sat and watched the waters rise, Len and I found that the insects did not like being submerged and had to tackle the hordes of centipedes and scorpions that were climbing up the bamboo supports. Using our wooden clompers, we knocked them back into the water but it was a losing battle. We could see the floods were rising higher by the minute and, it being obvious that the huts were no longer habitable, we moved to higher ground in the centre. There was no immediate space for us anywhere and it meant spending the night out in the open, but the next day accommodation was found in one of the newer huts.

After the floods had subsided our little group did not return to the evacuated huts, they were added to the hospital which now needed more space. As the railway work proceeded throughout the monsoon period at even greater pace large parties of sick, the prey of many diseases brought about by malnutrition and overwork, arrived daily by barge. They suffered in the main from bacilliary and amoebic dysentery; benign and malignant malaria; tropical ulcers; pellagra and beriberi. Most of them were seriously ill and some found to be dead in the barges, the journey having been too much of a strain. Early in July one such party brought the startling news that cholera had broken out in a camp at the Burmese end.

One of the world's most infectious diseases, it spread with great rapidity to all the many camps that now existed along the Kwai. Water borne, all bathing in the river was immediately prohibited and the use of water strictly controlled. Furthermore, the Japs were prevailed upon to issue supplies of chloride which was added to all water, whether for drinking or washing. Food was also disinfected in the same manner and cans of treated water provided at the meal queues to enable the dipping of mess tins and spoons. The high degree of chlorination made the meals even more unappetizing, but it was of course most necessary. All cases were isolated in special tented accommodation outside the boundaries, the brave doctors, medical orderlies and some volunteers staying there to treat them. A wasting disease, dehydration rapidly shrinks the body tissues and to counteract this it was imperative to pump saline liquid into the system continuously. For treatment some saline drips were manufactured and, in addition, the patients made to drink copious quantities of salt water - not an easy task when taking into consideration the vomiting and excretion common to the ailment. The white excretions were highly contagious and the men nursing and caring for the patients, constantly exposed to the disease, were deserving of the highest praise. It was all most fearsome, a companion could be quite well in the morning, develop a fever during the day and, after being reduced to a near skeleton, die that same night. Thanks to the sterling quality of the medical staff not all died, but unfortunately many hundreds up and down the line did so.

The Japanese and Koreans erected a barricade around their own quarters and spread a ring of chloride-of-lime on the ground along its perimeter. The outbreak of the epidemic really frightened them and instructions were issued for all victim's bodies to be burned. The Regimental Sergeant Major *(RSM of the Argyll & Sutherland Highlanders)*, Sandy Murdoch who was a tough Scot with a strong personality, volunteered to supervise the resulting funeral pyres - a gruesome duty. Extra fuel was now needed for the fires so additional working parties were sent out to collect bamboo *(the cookhouse already had their own collectors)* and I joined them. Before leaving the camp environs we were given wooden tags marked with Japanese characters, stood on a tray of permanganate of potash to disinfect our feet and then departed for the hillsides beyond the railway. Allowed by the guards to forage for ourselves we took as much advantage of the limited freedom as was possible, before returning the two or three miles with our heavy loads. It was on one of these forays that I had the opportunity of passing the shrine of the Surreys escapees and noticing how nicely the Thais were looking after it. Back in camp we repeated the disinfection process.

On the morning of the third day of my new employment we received startling news. When the food orderlies arrived with the breakfast pap they reported that five of the cooks had gone down with fevers overnight and had been transferred to the cholera isolation area. This was especially worrying and from now on, as each new day dawned, everybody wondered who would be next - it was almost akin to playing Russian Roulette. The fierceness of the epidemic even persuaded the Japs to pay heed, for once, to our doctors demands for assistance. Serum was issued for all to be inoculated, but for many it was too little too late. A Japanese medical contingent came and proceeded to take swabs from everybody; we lined up for the necessary glass rod insertion and those found to be positive cholera carriers sent into isolation. Even then our captors had an ulterior motive because, I was to learn when the war had been over for many years, prisoners of war in Korea, Manchuria and Northern China had been subject to the glass rod technique in a number of bizarre experiments in genetic engineering.

The cholera raged for three months, through the months of June, July and August, before finally petering out.

The barges bringing their dreadful loads of sick continued to arrive with passengers in the most appalling of condition. Most of them came late at night, landing at varying points along the river, and there was a nightly eerie procession of volunteers who had gone out to meet them and carry the worst cases to the hospital huts. Many were suffering from huge ulcers, usually on the shins, the result of a combination of those deadly bamboo thorns and the jungle conditions. In the tropical climate, with the lack of facilities for proper hygiene and the universal malnutrition, the original small sores rapidly developed into a deep ulcer. It was a major problem for the medics. Within a few days the wound would be the size of a ten pence piece and after a couple of weeks encompass the whole shin. Within a short space of time the ulcer ward occupied the whole hut and the doctors faced a daunting task, having by now exhausted the supplies of sulphonamide. Bandages for dressings were very scarce, the minimal quantity issued by the Japs being quite insufficient, and endeavouring to keep the ulcers as clean as possible was about all that could be done. The ward was a ghastly place, the stench of rotting flesh permeating the air, and it was not uncommon to see the medical orderlies rush outside to avoid vomiting, whereupon they returned refreshed to continue their nursing. A particularly gruesome duty was dealing with maggots. The myriads of flies that were ever present flocked to the open, rotting wounds to lay their eggs and the resulting maggots, together with putrefying flesh, had to be gouged out daily using ordinary spoons. It was an extremely painful and unpleasant experience for the patients, but vital to check the advance of gangrene. Soon more drastic measures were called for.

The man faced with the dilemma was Captain Markovitch, a Polish/Canadian serving with the Royal Army Medical Corps. He decided that the only means of saving the lives of the most seriously wounded was amputation. There was no operating theatre, only a limited amount of anaesthetic and only very few surgical instruments at his disposal. Preparations went ahead using a screened off section at the end of a hospital hut, whilst a group of specialist officers established a water distilling plant to provide purified water to sterilize the instruments. A Dutch chemist, who had for some time been experimenting with some plants grown in the surrounding countryside, co-operated with the surgeon and between them they evolved a suitable spinal anaesthetic. When everything was ready an orderly stood holding a large mirror just outside providing light by reflecting the rays of the sun down onto the operating area and the first operation commenced. It was a success and, the decision made, sixty more were carried out by the valiant captain over the next ten days. Unhappily they were not all successful, some of the patients having gone too far and had become too weak to survive the ordeal.

In due course many hundreds were to lose limbs, some below but mostly above the knee, and they occupied their own hut as a self sufficient 'Amput Battalion'. The later operations were performed under less primitive conditions when permission was eventually given, after much pressure from the doctors, for a separate hut to be converted for the purpose. More surgeons also arrived from up country, bringing additional surgical apparatus, which enabled other complaints to be dealt with by surgery.

In the wake of the gallant Markovitch's work came the need to make his limbless patients mobile. A group of able men applied their minds and skills to making, in the first instance, suitable crutches from the universal bamboo. Once they had provided the 'Amputs' with means of hopping about, devoted hands then went on with considerable improvisation to the manufacture of artificial limbs. Utilizing bamboo, bits of rubber tyres, sorbo from old motor seats, cut up sections of army water bottles and straps of webbing, perfectly adequate limbs evolved for use once stumps had healed. Our experts even made two half-size ones for a man who lost both legs, thereby helping him to learn to walk again. They carried on with the good work for the rest of our captivity and became sophis-

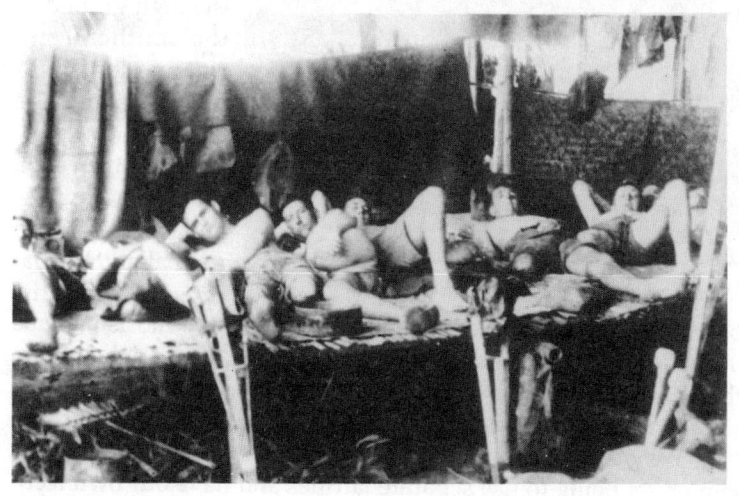

A group of amputs.

A double Amput.

The team who made the artificial limbs.

ticated enough to produce versions jointed at both the knee and ankle. It was a truly magnificent achievement.

All through the cholera period Len and I had been plagued with persistent diarrhoea. On the 23rd August we both reported sick and, as we had done on numerous previous occasions, provided stool tests *(not easy in our circumstances)* which provided to be positive EHB. This meant that our complaint was amoebic dysentery, which entailed our admission to a special isolation hut under the control of the hospital. So, the pair of us joined 200 others already installed in 'Amoebia Hall', a 100 metre long hut at the end of a line of seven on the high ground at the southern end running longitudinally from the camp central area. On the other side, an open space about the size of a football pitch separated us from the hospital huts; the first wards containing the avitaminosis patients which included those with beriberi and pellagra. Beyond them were others divided into the serious dysentery cases, malaria, surgical, skin and finally ulcer sections.

We were not completely cut off from the rest of the camp, the main object being to use separate latrines and have our own feeding points. Additionally, the doctors could keep a close check on

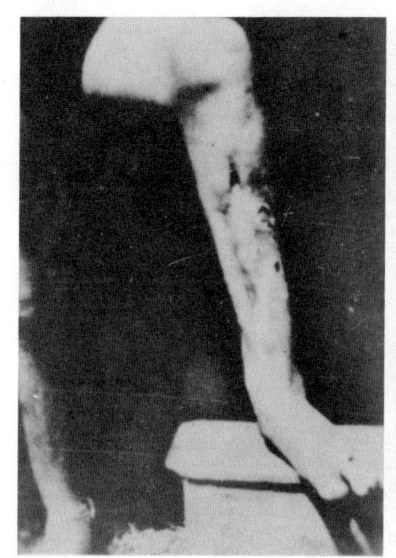

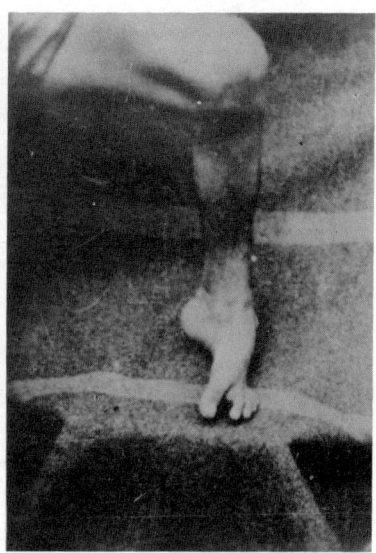

The ravages of tropical ulcers.

Amoebia Hall, sketched by S. Gimson from across the adjacent open space.

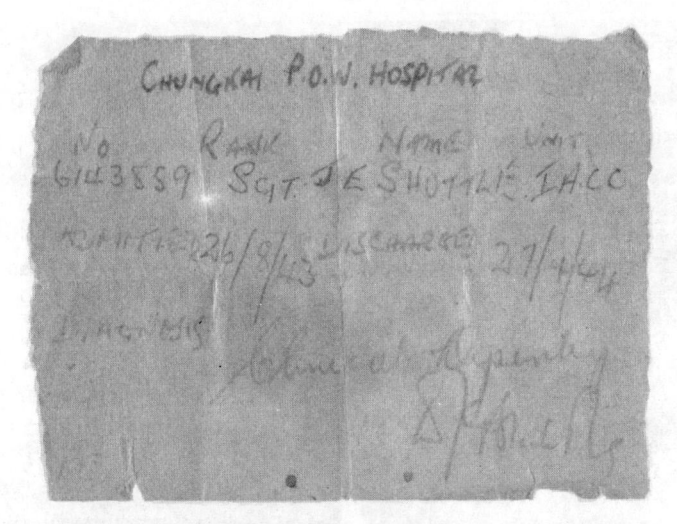

My hospital admission and discharge slip.

A general camp view.

any developments in our condition and anyone getting worse was transferred to the hospital proper for treatment. The only cure was the injection of emetine, a medicine extracted from the Ipecacuanha plant, but this was in very limited supply. Despite continued pressure from our doctors, the Japanese blatantly refused to heed their advice that the insidious disease could be brought under control with the drug. They argued that no amoebic dysentery existed and that it was just 'hill diarrhoea' which was not serious, so many people were allowed to die.

Settling in to our new surroundings, we soon established firm friendships with the other residents of the bay. They were Fred 'Wis' Wisbey from Enfield in North London; Charlie Beckett, a London Eastender from Walworth; Yorkshireman Colin 'Steve' Stevenson of Goole; 'Happy' Allen from Northampton and four Scotsmen. Two of the latter were Argyll Highlander Jock McLeod and 'Lanky' Roderick of the Lanarkshire Yeomanry. We all mixed very well and were to be together for the next eight months.

As the population of Chungkai grew so did the facilities. The improved operating theatre was built and, as up country camps completed their work on the railway, more surgeons and dentists arrived so a dental surgery was also opened. This gave me the opportunity to have my gums painted with some acriflavine, which checked an attack of gingivitis. Other improvements happened on the entertainment front as for the first time since leaving Changi organized concerts began, the prime mover being Eddie Edwins of the Medical Corps. He located some of the talented artistes from the Changi shows and produced a number of variety performances on an open bamboo platform between the hospital and Amoebia Hall. Eddie was the compere and our old friends Frankie and Bradfield provided the music for a string of singers, monologists and comedians. The current senior British officer, Lt. Col. Outram, a large man with a fine baritone voice, sang excerpts from the 'Maids of the Mountains' - a popular musical from the 1920s. On the lighter side was an excellent crooner, a professional in happier days with the Oscar Rabin Orchestra broadcasting band in London. For the shows he called himself Sammy Drayton, his stage name, but he was really Private Sid Short from Walworth and served in the same unit as Charlie Beckett.

After eighteen months in captivity, contact with the outside world remained nonexistence. No mail was received and no news from home had reached us but, although I personally was not aware of its location, a secret radio did operate. As detection would almost certainly have carried the death sentence for the operators, strict secrecy was absolutely essential so the fewer people aware of its whereabouts the better. Constructed within the false bottom of a standard army water bottle, the set was powered by batteries obtained and renewed by the audacious racketeers during their dangerous forays into Kanburi. Although others were involved, the main operators were the two Webber brothers, rubber planters from Malaya serving with the Federated States Volunteer Force, who listened in at a fixed time to the BBC. news being relayed from New Delhi in India. Whilst this was going on, fellow officers played bridge whilst the listeners tuned in down a hole dug below the sleeping platform. In addition, lookouts were casually posted as a further precaution should any sudden searches be imminent. As at Changi, any specific news of consequence was withheld for some weeks and then circulated mixed with fictional items; Captain Foulger, a former school master in Shanghai, usually broke the news to us.

Such radios existed in most of the other main camps and in general avoided discovery. The one exception was at Tamarkan, where two men who were caught received savage beatings, resulting in their deaths. It was an extremely dangerous and courageous undertaking and those so engaged, including the Webbers, received gallantry awards when they eventually came home. The latter returned to work in Malaya, one managing his rubber plantation and the other engaged in forestry, where they became involved in the insurrection suffered there during the 1950s.

Soon after moving in with the amoebics, Captain Foulger's news rumours included a reference to the Allied advances in the Mediterranean with the startling possibility of Sicily being invaded. Nobody could be sure of the fact, but what better way could there be than to make a disguised announcement from the stage in Eddie's Saturday night concert. He opened the performance by breaking into the refrain of a comic song called "Oh, Oh, Antonio" and that was sufficient confirmation; popular as he was, Eddie had probably never received so much applause. Of course there was still a long way to go but we now felt that, at last, the war was moving in our favour.

The many hundreds who used to attend these shows sat in a dense crowd on the ground. On one occasion someone in the centre felt what seemed to be snake under him, became panicky and at once tried to flee. This caused immediate pandemonium with people rushing about in all directions without really knowing why and within seconds we experienced the terror of stampeding. Some found themselves flying head first through the rickety atap of our adjacent hut and I went sprawling with countless others. It was all very strange - one just got carried along the tide. Fortunately nobody was hurt and afterwards a large pile of clompers that had been left behind in the rush waited to be retrieved.

Signalman Nash, our footballing despatch rider from Penang, arrived on one of the daily bargeloads of sick and was immediately sent to the avitaminosis ward. Poor Nash was now a pathetic figure, so skeletal that I had difficulty in recognizing him as he weakly hailed me; no amount of persuasion would induce him to eat and each day his condition deteriorated. Within a few days when I made my usual afternoon visit he was unconscious and breathing in a laboured manner. By morning this former strong and powerful man was dead. He hailed from Heston in Middlesex and I am reminded of him each year when I see the memorium that his family have inserted in the local press regularly on the anniversary of his birth.

All of our little group in Amoebia Hall had, like myself, many comrades coming into the camp hospital and we endeavoured to visit them daily. One of the main effects of their various diseases was loss of appetite, which in turn worsened their condition, so we took along our 'doovers' garnished with tamarind and lime marmalade to tempt them. Sometimes it worked, but unfortunately it was mostly of little avail.

Throughout the later stages of 1943 the development of Chungkai was truly incredible. It was always the policy of the Japanese to leave all administration in our own hands, which was just as well because I have never experienced so disorganized a race. We had the benefit of many able, well-trained officers who quickly produced order out of chaos and one in particular, Major Marsh, was a very strong personality. Bullying our captors to provide his needs, he negotiated the closing of the poor original canteen and obtained permission to establish one under our own management. Supplies were purchased from Boon Pong, a pro-British Thai contractor based in Kanburi, and the project was run by a canteen committee. It was named the PRI, the initials of the President of the Regimental Institute which is the title of the welfare officer in each British Army battalion. Most of the customers were, of course, the fortunate paid officers who were able to enhance their diet; the majority of other ranks in the camp were sick and therefore without pay, so we could only sit and watch. There were some who still had valuables for sale and others who had just arrived from the working parties also had money left that they had not been able to spend up country. Still more earned a little by acting as batmen, if you please, to the affluent officers.

The officers contribution to the welfare fund was, though, very welcome and it ensured extra food being made available to the heavy sick. I benefited when symptoms of beriberi appeared and I reported my suspicions to Major Black, the Indian Medical Services doctor who had admitted me to the amoebic section. He tested my reflexes on the knees and ankles, neither of them responding, and then pressed his thumb into the flesh around my shins to leave a definite indentation. These were sure signs that I was now in the early stages and he prescribed a daily dose of liquid yeast and one duck egg per day for two weeks, the latter being courtesy of the welfare fund. Apart from arresting the beriberi, the eggs were a sheer luxury for me; after collecting each one every day I visited the cook-house and boiled it in a kerosene can on one of their fires. On the few times when this was not convenient I wandered around the camp until I came across anyone having a private 'cook-up' and borrowed theirs. Once boiled I ate it held in the hand, after having chopped the top off, with my one and only dessert spoon. At the end of the two weeks the swellings had gone and so there were no more duck eggs - I did miss them and whenever I did manage to obtain a little money it was spent on them. A life saver then, we are now told that they are dangerous due to the cholesterol content.

October 1943 saw the completion of the railway, astonishingly within one year of our arrival in Thailand. The Burmese groups and our own workers met at Konkuita, twenty miles inside the Thai border and a special ceremony took place for the laying of the final and connecting track. The Japanese media was there with newsreel cameras recording the event for consumption at home, but there were no ragged, starving P.O.W.s in sight. They had sent to various camps to locate the fittest men, mostly cooks who had had the benefit of larger rations, and fitted them out in new clothing!

That day everybody in all camps along the line received a treat. With much aplomb, each man was given two pineapple cubes - "Tojo presentoes", we were told. A similar gift was given each year on the Emperor's birthday!

CHAPTER 12.

BULGING CHUNGKAI.

Construction work now completed, the fitter men were soon evacuated from the north. In addition to the rest of our own No. 2 Group, large batches from the others, including some of the Australians and Dutch from Burma, joined us and the greatly enlarged camp was separated into the 'Blue' area for the able-bodied; 'Light' sick and 'Heavy' sick, the latter being the hospital section. The whole came under the command of the senior British officer, now Lt. Col. Williamson, and by the end of the year the population had reached 10,000. With so many people within its boundaries, the organization to turn the camp into a community continued apace and the place was unrecognizable to those who had left it to go up the line at the beginning of the year.

There was, for instance, the Taylor Hairdressing Emporium. Run by a Sergeant Taylor of the Norfolk Regiment, the salon was located on the open ground between the old defunct Jap controlled canteen and Amoebia Hall. Prior to enlisting, he had been employed as manager of the hairdressing department in London at the Regent Palace Hotel and now lost no time in gathering together a group of fellow professionals to go into business. A number of tree trunks were placed in a circle to act as the barber's chairs and bamboo stools knocked up for furnishing the waiting area under the nearby trees. The many officers blessed with a regular income provided him with plentiful custom, at five cents for either a shave or a haircut; in fact monthly season tickets were available which entitled the holder to a daily shave and two haircuts. The lofty Taylor rarely performed himself, ushering his customers to the barber of their choice, and it was indeed a rare honour when he deemed to do so.

I had first met the man in Wun Lun and he had remained with us at both Tarkilen and Wampo South. Several years my senior, he had recalled how he had gone with some friends and show business customers to enlist in a sudden bout of patriotism. Before going to the Regent Palace he had spent some time in Hollywood, working as a make-up man for the Max Factor company. Likeable as he was I felt that perhaps his tales erred him on the side of the romantic, but it was wrong of me to doubt him. A year or two after the war I visited the hotel and there, in its salon, was the inimitable Mr. Taylor. Resplendently attired in elegant black jacket and striped trousers, he was ushering the clients in with as much aplomb as ever.

A considerable number of talented entertainers arrived with the influx to supplement Eddie and his friends. Their combination saw the emergence of the Chungkai Theatre, where regular shows were produced up to the middle of 1944. Taking advantage of a natural bowl in the vicinity of the cook-house, where the ground rose fairly steeply away from the river, an earthen stage was built at the bottom end and then the hillside was hewn into rows of benches, creating an auditorium seating several thousands. Next came the stage and, using the ever adaptable bamboo and atap, it was roofed in, flies were erected and there was even a proscenium arch. The bamboo wings were reversible, utilizing cleverly made hinges *(again from bamboo)* that made it possible to have a boxed or winged stage. Lighting was provided by some paraffin lanterns that our redoubtable friend Major Marsh the quartermaster had extracted from the

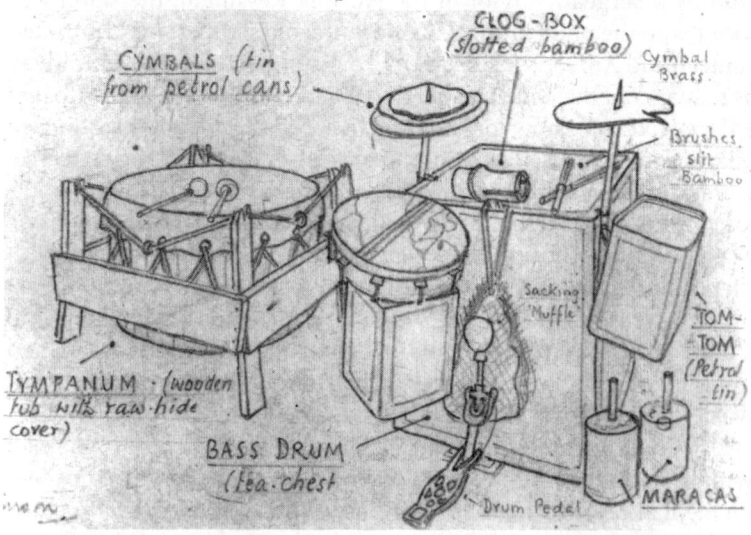

The camp made percussion set.

Japs. Between the stage and the first row of earthen seats was the orchestra pit, there being by now enough musicians to provide music from a variety of instruments. The two guiding stars in this field were Norman Smith, a rotund Yorkshireman from Halifax who in normal times was an organist, and Eric Cliffe, a music teacher.

Norman was a fellow resident in Amoebia Hall who specialized in the light music side of the entertainment. He formed an orchestra of about ten players and among them were the talented Lance Corporal Bradfield from the East Surreys with his cornet; a Dutch/Japanese wizard on the piano accordion called Sabatini *(Frankie having moved on elsewhere)*; two guitarists, four violinists, a bass player and finally a drummer.

The body of the double bass was made out of odd pieces of teak and plywood, whilst the strings were mainly telephone wires smuggled in by a signalman who had been employed erecting the overhead lines along the railway. A whole medley of gadgets improvised on an old tea-chest served as the percussion set, a kerosene can became a tom-tom; tin cut from other kerosene cans were the cymbals; split bamboo served for the brushes and a simple piece of slotted bamboo acted as a clog box. The only genuine items were a well worn side-drum, that had been diligently lugged up to Thailand by its owner, and a drum pedal that was muffled by rice sacking. Finally there was a tympanum which used rawhide - from one of the slaughtered water buffaloes - stretched over a wooden tub.

Orchestrations had to be memorised and Norman, in the next bay to me, spent many hours writing the arrangements with the aid of a guitar. In addition he composed some original songs for the various shows and it was fascinating watching him writing the music down with consummate ease. Paper was an almost nonexistent commodity, but he somehow seemed to obtain sufficient to write out the necessary band parts.

Eric Cliffe was also busy in another part of the camp and, adding even more musicians to Norman's ten, gave a series of Promenade concerts. Finding some more strings and clarinetists, he was able to lead an orchestra twenty strong who gave us extracts from Schubert, Mozart and Elgar. Singing with them was Captain James Clark, a Scottish doctor with a fine tenor voice, whose repertoire included Pucini's 'Your tiny hand is frozen' from La Boheme. 'Where-e'er you walk' was another favourite. The Dutch formed a choir and they too joined in with the orchestra, especially at Christmas time.

Some of the players also performed jazz concerts as the Swing Sextet with bandsman Bradfield leading them with his cornet.

It was towards the end of the year that I first met Jack Griffin. Whilst attending the newly established skin clinic to be treated for another outbreak of sores, I was attended to by a talkative little orderly who told me that he hailed from Staines in Middlesex. He lived only three miles or so from me and indeed had worked at the local Gas Company which was next door to the Waterworks where I was employed. However we were strangers but now became good friends, remaining together for the rest of our captivity. Jack was a member of the St. Johns Ambulance Brigade, which gained him entry into the Royal Army Medical Corps, and he had come to Malaya with the initial Brigade of the 18th Division in January 1942. Posted to Alexandria Military Hospital he had survived the dreadful massacre by having been on the second floor, locking himself in one of the lavatories in the corridor and staying there until the Japanese troops had departed on the following day. It was a nerve-racking experience as he could hear the rampaging soldiers outside and could see their feet under the door.

Ches and Gunner Irwin turned up, the latter having found himself in Group 4, and when I introduced them to Jack it was quite a gathering of local boys so far away from home. Soon we discovered yet another one.

Making the daily visitation to the river for our ablutions we were greeted by a crowd of men from the newly arrived Group 4 people. They were splashing about in the middle, the water being at its lowest ebb and was almost fordable, and one of them was vaguely familiar. At school there had been two Butler brothers and, although I had not seen them for some ten years, I decided that I had met Ken. Upon approaching I learned that I was wrong - it was the other brother, Cecil. He was in the Beds and Herts and, like Jack Griffin, had come out with the 18th Division. Neither he nor Gunner stayed long before going on to Tamarkan, which was the base camp of their No. 4 Group, and then moving back down to Singapore en route for Japan. On the sea voyage they were the victims of torpedoing by the United States Navy and both spent many hours in the water after their ship was sunk with heavy loss of life. Some survivors were eventually picked up by another Japanese vessel and my two friends were among them, finally arriving in Japan to spend the rest of their captivity at work in a coal mine.

A fair number of the East Surreys were now in the camp, but none of the original draft who had accompanied me to Shanghai were among them. I had also become separated from my companions of 2nd Echelon, now that the only one who had been with me here, Holly Hollyman, had left for Kanburi. 'Lakri' Wood had died in Chungkai when I was still at Wampo South and 'Lottie' Collins perished in Tarsao. The latter was a veteran Warrant Officer of over twenty years service who had been my boss at 2nd Echelon, having joined Command HQ from India in 1939. He had, at that time, been allowed to bring his wife with him on the posting and she had left Singapore only a few days before capitulation. No news of her fate was ever received by Lottie and it was only after release that I learned that her ship, like the majority of the evacuees, had gone down shortly after sailing with no survivors.

The residents of Amoebia Hall continued to increase and we became more crowded than ever. At first we had been able to spread our wings a little, but we were soon back to the old cramped conditions of just about two feet per man. Furthermore the loose bamboo slats on the sleeping platform had again become infested with bed bugs and body lice - we thought these had been eliminated with the destruction of the old huts. Removal of the slats for cleaning regularly limited the bed bugs activities but they soon returned. Similarly it was necessary to constantly go through the seams of our sparse clothing and crack the lice eggs with our thumb nails. Another nuisance were crab-lice, a most unpleasant affliction, which attacked me in a very strange fashion. Developing an uncomfortable film over my eyes which from time to time seemed to move, I consulted my medical orderly friend Jack who told me that my eye lashes were infested. To get rid of the pests *(they really do look like a tiny crab)* he delicately cut off both of my lashes and told me to shave off my pubic hair and also under the armpits. Greaves the barber duly obliged.

I pondered mostly on our plight at night time as I prepared myself for the coming night's rest. Trying to get into the most suitable position squeezed between two fellow souls, I endeavoured to ward off the dive bombing mosquitoes by curling up under my half blanket; my aluminium mess tin wrapped in what few clothes I still possessed acted as a pillow. The bed bugs though kept biting and often I would be awoken by a great big fat grey louse crawling across my face. On such nights I longed for the joy of immersing in a warm luxuriant bath, then changing into nice clean pyjamas and climbing into a bed between gleaming white sheets!

The companionship of the small group in our bay helped as we all made the best of the situation. We talked for hours of our differing lives and customs back home and occasionally, when the mood took us, had a quiet little sing-along. The Loch Lomond Air was sung to the refrain of 'On the muddy, bloody banks of Kanburi', whilst a popular song of the 1930s 'Buddy can you spare me a dime?' evoked the apt parody of 'Once I built a railroad to Bangkok, made it race against time'. There was also a song, well known to all who served in Malaya, whose origin was in some doubt. It was reputedly written by a Scottish soldier before the outbreak of hostilities, but no-one was sure. Titled 'The moon is shining o'er Malaya', the lyrics were:-

"Palm trees are swaying in the sunset
Casting their shadows o'er the sea.
What's going on in the moonlight?
Stay awhile and listen with me.

For the moon is shining o'er Malaya
The stars they twinkle down from up above.
Girls in the sarongs and their kebayas
In Kampongs sing their songs of love.

You can hear terangbulan and old serina,
Songs their mothers sang in days gone by.
From Penang to Ipoh and Malacca
You can hear those sweet enchanting lullabies.

You can hear those guitars strumming in the moonlight
For the echo of their kerongchongs never die.
For the moon is shining o'er Malaya
And to think we've got to leave it bye and bye."

Wis was in the Beds and Herts and we now had another member of his battalion in the hut. He was Stan Henderson who happened to have very left wing political views, so we had many friendly arguments. Such was his fervour that he endeavoured to organize a camp Communist Party and actually conducted meetings at our rear in the bamboo thickets. I have heard of him twice since the war, the first occasion being in 1946 when there was much dissatisfaction in London among returning servicemen looking for living accommodation. Large blocks of luxury flats standing empty were taken over by squatters in a mass demonstration and the event attracted much attention nationally. The name of the movement's leader was emblazoned in the newspaper headlines and who should it be but Stan. Thirty nine years passed before he came to my notice again. It was in 1985 in a television documentary programme when one of the interviewees was expounding his political views and, although this person had long white locks of hair together with white side-whiskers as opposed to the tall young blonde man I remembered, there was still no doubt regarding his identity. Our Stanley was still pursuing his views completely unchanged from long ago.

With the Chungkai theatre now ready, Eddie Edwins had the luxury of putting his shows on there. One of his newest recruits was Bobby Spong, a private in the Royal Ordnance Corps, who was a really excellent female impersonator. The son of a Chelsea publican, he had been an entertainer before capture and had been able to retain some of his professional props of women's attire. Additionally, with the help of some of his friends, he made more costumes by sewing together odd scraps of material and mosquito nets. Consequently Bobby was able to 'ring the changes' in each show, whether singing comic songs like "I'm one of the ruins that Cromwell knocked about a bit" or taking the leading role in a Musical. He was a very talented performer.

Another newcomer was Eddie Monkhouse, a very professional singer, who soon became a regular performer at the theatre.

Christmas 1943 was a memorable affair, events taking on a carnival atmosphere. Our second festive season 'behind the wire', it also marked the end of a truly dreadful year with the railway slavery behind us. There were still to be many harrowing times ahead but at the moment, and on that day, we were thankful for the lull. As on the previous year, the cooks performed miracles and produced something really special. Extra portions of sugar came with morning pap, plus a piece of rice bread; at lunch time there was even stew with the normal plain rice but the evening meal surpassed anything we had ever seen. It consisted of a very thick stew, heavily mixed with yam, pumpkin, marrow, Chinese radish, cucumber and kachanghijau. For sweet there was a larger than normal doover well garnished with tamarind jam. Our group did even better. An enterprising fellow had stolen a duck from the Japanese and had raffled it, fully roasted, at 5 cents a ticket. Len held the winning number and we sat outside in the thicket and devoured it by hand - I can still visualize him pulling the bird to pieces and passing the portions around.

A race track had been marked off in the open area facing us, Taylors Salon having closed for the day, complete with a paddock for the 'horses' to parade around; there was also a 'ring' where the bookies *(mostly Australian)* set up stalls. The 'horses' were selected from the strongest and most powerful men available, carrying small light men on their backs as jockeys. During the morning a great race meeting took place, a full race card being carried out in as realistic a manner as possible, each entrant even being sponsored by an owner. The opening ceremony was performed by Bobby in his best finery complete with lacy hat, escorted by Mark Ross resplendent in full grey morning dress and topper. It was another of the theatrical props that seemed to be conjured up like magic in that remote area.

One of the winning participants was 'Weary' Dunlop. An Australian Lieutenant Colonel surgeon, he was one of the most popular men in any of the camps in Thailand, who had recently come down from the Burma section to take charge of the constantly growing hospital. Of deceptively laconic appearance which many thought gave rise to his nickname *(it was actually a play on Dunlop, the tyre manufacturers, hence 'tired')*, this 6ft. 3in. giant of a man had already become something of a legend. All through the speedo period he had argued fiercely with the Japs over their policy of forcing the sick men to work, but to no avail as both he and his fellow doctors were constantly overruled. One of Weary's answers was to accompany the working parties, having previously arranged that certain very ill people should fake 'faint' en route at prearranged points. He would then pick the first one up, put him over his shoulder and run him back to camp, completely disregarding whatever fuss the guards made.

A brilliant surgeon, he carried out hundreds of successful operations during the captivity. On all occasions copious medical notes were compiled - he insisted on being provided with paper for this purpose - and this information was of very considerable help to the medical authorities upon repatriation. The numerous colostomy cases in particular benefited in this regard. Awarded the O.B.E. for his services as a prisoner of war, Weary became an eminent Australian and International consultant surgeon and was knighted as Sir Edward Dunlop, GMC, OBE. In 1977 he was voted Australian Man of the year and as a very active eighty-year old, travelled to London in 1985 and again in 1987. I had pleasure of meeting him again at the Far East POW reunion at London's Festival Hall during these visits, when he received a standing ovation from the 2000 present.

All in all, that Christmas of 1943 was a pronounced success, ending quietly as the Dutch choir toured the camp singing carols. The following morning we faced reality again as still more of the dreadful barge loads of very sick and dying men arrived.

A case of Beriberi...

Typical living quarters.

Mealtime.

CHAPTER 13.

1944 AND STILL AT CHUNGKAI.

As we approached the second anniversary of capture, we had still not received any communication whatsoever from home. It was about this time that I awoke one morning to the memory of a most vivid dream. In it I was back at Wun Lun and walking down the lane towards the Thai market stalls, but as I neared them the scenery changed and I found myself in other more familiar surroundings. I was now actually going down another lane that led into the High Street of my home town and there, sitting on chairs watching the passing traffic, were all of my own and fiancee's families. They greeted me as though it were a perfectly normal way to meet and everybody was intrigued by the strange clothing I was wearing, especially the huge blue patches on my tattered khaki drill trousers. My clompers, too, were of great interest and there was much comment about the moustache I had only started to grow after capture. Animated conversations were held as I passed round some banana fritters on banana leaves just purchased, which were accepted without comment. After a short while I made my apologies and bade them goodbye, pointing out that it was nearly six o'clock and we were not allowed by the Japs to be in the market after this hour. So evocative was this dream that it has remained crystal clear in my mind ever since.

The strange thing about this incident was that shortly afterwards rumours started circulating that some mail had arrived in the camp. Following such a long period of complete isolation, this news was greeted with great excitement and there was much joyousness when the rumour was confirmed. There ensued a long delay in ultimate distribution, our captors insisting that each letter must be censored by the camp interpreter; as his knowledge of written English was very limited only a handful were released daily. Eventually the system was speeded up, after pressure from the British commanding officer, but many of the mailbags that arrived in Thailand never left the Jap stores. Working parties reported seeing them in a deteriorated condition and showing signs of having been attacked by rats.

It was some weeks before I was lucky enough to receive anything and then my name was called. There were three whole letters for me, one from my father and the other two from Joan. Neither of them had any idea where I was nor even if I had survived the defence of Singapore, but they had responded to advice to address the letters to the International Red Cross for onward transmission. Although eighteen months old they were a great joy to receive, even though they highlighted the cruelty of the Japanese in not advising anyone any details of their prisoners. My father wrote:

"Egham,
27/7/42.

My Dear Jack,
    Still with no news I am rather lost for words. Anyway praying that you will receive this some day, I will start by hoping it will find you as well as we can expect. No words of mine will alter facts and I'm afraid we must just grin and bear it.

    I am very pleased to say that we received the letter you wrote on January 12th 1942 and that Joan hers also. She and Mother take things fine, they are just waiting for the time when we shall all be together again.

    We all know that things must be pretty bad for you, but I think you will take it.

    We are all fairly well at home at present, Lily and her baby Joey are back home with us again and Ivy's Dick is somewhere in the Middle East.

    Well son I am not writing much as there is only a chance that this will reach you. We know nothing at all about you except that you are posted missing.

    I do so hope that this will find you somewhere and that you will be able to write to us. We have waited for SUCH a long time for news.

There is nothing more I can say, son, except to tell you to take it like a man. It will be all over one day so, wishing you all the best possible, I remain,
Your loving Dad.

XXXXXXX From Mum and all at home.
X From Joey with love."

From this time on I received a few other letters spasmodically until they were curtailed, the Japs having told the Red Cross in 1943 that full letters could no longer be accepted. Any further communications would have to be on one page only, with the text printed in script which was not to exceed twenty five words. The first one which came to hand was from Joan and it read:

"Wed. January 5th. 1944.
JACK DARLING,
CARD RECEIVED. VERY RELIEVED. EVERYONE HERE WELL. HOPE YOU ARE. DON'T WORRY ABOUT ANYTHING. ALWAYS THINKING OF YOU. GOD BLESS.
LOVE EVER.
JOAN."

The card referred to was the one I had been able to send in November 1942, which eventually arrived home in January 1944 and it was only then that they learned of my survival of the Malayan Campaign. The communication also gave my location at No.2 Group in Thailand, which speeded up delivery times. Nevertheless it was taking up to eight months or more for the abbreviated letters to reach us and, as they were rationed to one per month, most of those sent in 1945 were arriving after I was homeward bound!

With 10,000 people now concentrated in Chungkai a local economy began to evolve. Occasionally it was possible to make a few Ticals, the cigarette industry being one such instance. The ready made varieties Red Bull and Sheaf had long since disappeared, but locally grown tobacco was still available for purchase. It was only partially cured and fearfully strong and I personally had by now opted to stop smoking, but others felt differently. So there was always a steady demand, to meet which the Amputs turned their hut into a hive of industry with the formation of the Amput Cigarette

```
Cas/80/767                          Infantry Record Office,
                                    Stanwell Road School,
                                    ASHFORD, Middlesex.

Mr. A. Shuttle,                              4th July, 1944.
"Ferndene"
2, Limes Road,
EGHAM, Surrey.
```

Sir,

    I thank you for forwarding the Prisoner of War card you have received from your Son, No. 6143899 Serjeant Jack Frederick SHUTTLE, The East Surrey Regiment, details of which have been recorded. I would advise you to address your letters as follows:-

    PRISONER OF WAR POST.   SERVICE DES PRISONNIERS DE GUERRE.

    No. 6143899 Serjeant Jack Frederick SHUTTLE
    British Prisoner of War,
    No. 2 P.O.W. Camp, Thailand,
    c/o Japanese Red Cross,
    TOKYO, Japan.

    Your letters should be clearly written and should not exceed twenty five words not including addresses.

    The prisoner of war card is returned herewith, together with an official notification, recording him a Prisoner of War.

    I am, Sir,
    Your obedient servant,

    Major
for Officer in Charge of Records.

I am finally officially reported Prisioner-of-War, July 1944.

No. Cas/ /
(If replying, please quote above No.)

Army Form B. 104—83A

Infantry Record Office,

ASHFORD, Middlesex.

Station.

4th July 19 44

SIR ~~OR MADAM~~,

I have to inform you that a report has been received from the War Office to the effect that (No.) 6143833 (Rank) Serjeant (Name) Jack Frederick SHUTTLE (Regiment) The East Surrey Regiment is a Prisoner of War in Japanese hands, No. 2 POW Camp, Thailand

Should any other information be received concerning him, such information will be at once communicated to you.

Instructions as to the method of communicating with Prisoners of War can be obtained at any Post Office.

I am,

SIR ~~or Madam~~,

Your obedient Servant,

Mr. A. Shuttle,
"Ferndene" 2 Limes Road,
EGHAM, Surrey.

Officer in charge of Records.

IMPORTANT.—Any change of your address should be immediately notified to this Office. It should also be notified, if you receive information from the soldier above, that his address has been changed.

> WEDNESDAY. JANUARY. 5th
> 1944.
> JACK DARLING.
> CARD RECEIVED. VERY RELIEVED. EVERYONE HERE WELL. HOPE you ARE. DON'T WORRY ABOUT ANYTHING. ALWAYS THINKING OF you. GOD BLESS.
> LOVE EVER.
> JOAN.

My first twenty-five word letter from Joan.

Company. Having obtained supplies of tobacco the manufacturers were in constant need of thin paper, in particular the very fine quality texture found in bibles. Its pages could be profitably sold and Bill Johnson, who was a devout Salvationist, resisted parting with his for quite a long period. Eventually, though, he decided that he would be forgiven his sin in the name of survival and joined in the trade with the rest. Some Australians were very adept at peeling off thin layers of paper from old postcards, but generally carefully washed newspapers were used. They were prewar American ones retrieved from the stores where they had been the wrappings for dry rations. The purpose was thus served, even though sometimes the whole cigarette would go up in flames.

Salesmen were employed to go around the camp plying their wares, which were offered in bundles of five. On show nights they were in attendance at the theatre, with trays slung around their necks in the traditional manner. The smokers had to manage without matches, it being the custom to go to the cook-house and light up from its fires. The alternative was to ask for a light from passing fellow smokers.

The cobblers were another profitably active group. Supervised by a grizzly Australian first world war veteran called Skipper, a number of men went into business making sandals. Their raw material came from the water buffaloes which provided our meat, the hides being hung up to dry on bamboo frames. After curing, the team cut the skins into dry sections and converted them into attractive, well made sandals - made to measure if one wished. Skipper, too, engaged a number of salesmen and did good business amongst the officers. Unfortunately, although the sandals looked good, they proved to be a little uncomfortable owing to the leather not being properly cured.

Still more volunteers went round offering various concoctions and we even saw the revival of the 'hot, sweet and filthy' coffee. A Dutchman named Englander hit upon the idea of buying bananas and spring onions at the canteen, which he chopped up and then mashed to create a palatable dressing. Choosing meal times to make his rounds, he did a roaring trade at 5 cents a portion.

Communities of the size to which we had grown usually have their complement of criminals and we were no exception. A series of raids by a blanket stealing gang, who stooped low enough to rob the sick whilst they slept, prompted members of the Corps of Military Police to reorganize. One of their captains was appointed Provost Marshall, who quickly introduced vigilante patrols. This action resulted in the culprits being arrested, found guilty and sentenced to detention in a special area under the control of the MPs. Therefore it had become necessary to have a prison within a prison. Although the worst excesses had now been brought under control there was still a certain amount of individual thieving going on, as I was to discover to my cost.

Going down the river one afternoon with Len and Wis for our daily wash, on arrival I placed my clothes in a neat little pile on the bank. My companions were only wearing their 'Jap-Happies', but I had on my smart green Dutch army shorts, with a belt which was a webbing strap removed from my haversack. In the pockets were my one and only handkerchief in a distinctive multicoloured pattern, plus a small stub of pencil. Folding the shorts carefully, I placed them over my clompers and laid the tattered remains of a towel on the top. Upon returning we could find no trace of them. They had been stolen and I stood there with not a stitch of clothing to my name.

Len remarked that the lads in the hut would fix something up for me, so there was nothing for it but to dry myself in the sun and put up with the indignity of walking the quarter of a mile back through the camp in my naked state.

When we had arrived Len had produced the remains of his shorts, which were in tatters apart from the waistband and crotch, and loaned them to me until other arrangements could be made. A meeting was convened to discuss my problem, at which Charlie Beckett mentioned that he knew a Dutch tailor who could probably be persuaded to make a pair of shorts. All he would need would be the material and one Tical cash. Jock McLeod then said that there was a man further down the hut still in possession of an army canvas kitbag and was sure he would part with it for a reasonable sum. Off Jock went to find him and returned with an agreement, after some haggling, to let us have the bag for fifty cents. Now we had to find $1.50 and a count round revealed that the ten could barely raise this amount between us, which in any event would leave everybody out of pocket. The answer was my treasured bush hat, which for some time had been much admired by my Dutch friend, Englander. It was without its pugri and hatband, removed due to bug infestation, but he was prepared to pay the amount required. So I did a deal. Jock soon bought the kit bag, made of thick canvas in dark blue with the name Gunner Stevenson painted on the side in white letters, and off it went to the tailor. He started work immediately, opening it out into a flat piece of material and shredding strands from the edge for sewing. Within a few days the article was finished, with a ruffled waist with a strip threaded through to act as a belt. They really were a most excellent pair of shorts, despite being decorated by the fragmented letters of the original owner's name. Becoming stiff when immersed in water they proved easy to launder and served me well throughout the remaining years.

I returned the tattered shorts to Len and I was extremely grateful to him and the rest of my friends for their unselfish support. I did miss my hat, though.

Still without any footwear since the loss of my clompers, it was necessary to go barefoot for some while until I was able to scrounge some more kapok wood and a strip of rubber to replace them. With no towel drying had to be by standing in the sun, until one day my missing handkerchief came to light. It was about one month after the incident that Wis was visiting a friend from his battalion in the blue area and saw it hanging up to dry in a nearby bedspace. The colours were so varied and bold that he was in no doubt about it being mine and came hurrying back to tell me of his discovery. He rushed in shouting out that he had found the thieving bastard, so I went back with him and quietly walked through the hut in question to confirm his opinion. He was right and we immediately went across to see the Provost Marshall, to whom I had previously reported my loss. Two military policemen called on the man occupying the bed-space concerned and searched his kit, which included the stub of pencil and my webbing strap as well as the hanky. He was promptly arrested and removed to the detention centre, where I was requested to attend for identification purposes. My lovely green shorts and the clompers were not recovered, having been sold long since. I never learned the man's name, but apparently he was a persistent thief and other stolen items were also found in his possession. He was duly locked up in the detention centre for an indefinite period.

Jock McLeod found himself in trouble with one of the Koreans when he was hastily summoned "Kurrah, Buggairo" for not bowing in passing. In truth he had not seen the guard and tried to explain, but his excuses were ignored. This led to the fiery Glaswegian losing his temper and a torrent of abuse poured from his lips, which was not abated by the usual blows to the head. Eventually several other guards rushed to the scene, overpowering poor Jock and dragging him to the guardhouse. After an initial beating, it was decided that he should be objected to the Oriental symbol of disgrace, i.e. 'losing face', so a notice was hung from his neck stating that he must obey commands at all times. A musician was sent for and the pair were made to walk around the camp for all to witness. Jock and the rest of us had the last laugh, though, because our old pal Bradfield had come forward with his cornet and played the Colonel Bogey March!

Jock had really upset the Japs and the above farce was followed by two weeks in the 'no good house', a small building of bamboo and atap just a few feet high and wide. There was insufficient room to stand up or lie down and prisoners so confined experienced the most uncomfortable conditions, being given no access to daylight nor allowed out to perform bodily functions. Finally, the only food provided was one basic meal of cold, sour rice with a little tea, which was pushed through the door each day. Jock completed his sentence without complaint and, amoebic dysentery or not, soon recovered to his old tough self.

Padre Webb, a Presbyterian minister from Malaya, had for some time been pressing for a centre to conduct church services. When enough materials had come to hand, thanks to his efforts, a universal place of worship came into being affording facilities for all religious faiths to take part. It was an open ended building, the congregations sitting on the ground in front of the covered-in transept; Catholics, Anglicans, Nonconformists and Dutch protestants all taking turns to attend their separate services. Len and I came as often as possible, favouring those conducted by the popular Padre Webb or the equally well liked Australian Padre Thorpe, and it was here in this haven of peace that we found peace and tranquillity. Our life was so PUBLIC. At other times, in an endeavour to divorce ourselves from the constant company of the many thousands surrounding us, we liked to take a stroll most evenings around the mile and a quarter of perimeter fence. Len and I became very close during these years and took strength from each other.

Drawn by S. Gimson.

Sick parties continued to arrive from up country and the hospital remained as full as ever. Many men suffered with extreme dermatitis. Visits to the skin ward saddened me to see so many reduced to skeletal proportions and covered with large, scaly, festering patches all over their bodies; the elbows, shoulders and hips being particularly affected. The cause was an advanced form of pellagra and dry beriberi, the latter bringing much discomfort to the limbs, especially the feet, with nagging neuritic pains. Some tried to get relief by walking about at night, whilst others slept with their feet immersed in a bowl of water.

The malaria wards, too, were over-full with malignant terpia cases. This form of the disease often develops into a cerebral spinal version, which was usually fatal and caused much agony. The afflicted howled throughout the nights like mad dogs and died the most frightening of deaths.

An acquaintance from Temple Hill days, a Corporal Smith of the Royal Signals, came down from Kanu on one of these parties. It had been one of the more notorious camps some 100 kilometres north and his experiences there had been so appalling that one of his companions, Sgt. Pilot Mac Johnstone, was moved to write the following poem;

"KANU 2."

There's a ghostly camp of horrors to the north of Kanu 2,
There are scores of bamboo crosses in the mud.
And they mark the place where thousands lie
where once the jungle grew,
in the rest that was denied them when they lived.

It was known what men could do by the docs at Kanu 2,
That the pace was hot and it was bound to tell.
So they warned the yellow cranks of the thinning of the ranks
and the colonels made a fuss about it too.

Men had striven hard and long with a courage that was strong,
That they had died from overwork was plain to all.
Some were barely twenty-one and arrangements had begun
to bury them as they received the call.

The doctors raved and stormed as the gory total grew
but the yellow monsters sneered at all they said.
The blank reply was simply that the railway must go through,
even though the place was filled with British dead.

Then the rains began to fall and the working party, small,
had to work as they had never worked before.
And they had to walk for miles through the deeply cut defiles
where the yellow swine for ever drove them more.

They returned to camp at dark looking haggard, worn and stark,
their backs and aching shoulders fiery red.
They were fed on jungle stew and t'was all that they could do
to drag their weary bodies off to bed.

They awoke before the dawn, even hope had almost gone,
then they thought of stricken comrades who had fell.
And when daylight trickled through you could see the weary crew
as they ploughed along the muddy road to hell.

On a still tropic night, with the death rate at its height,
the living, aching suffering prayed to God.
But no succour came until that awful rail went through.
T'was the vengeance of the little yellow 'god'.

There's a ghostly camp of horrors to the north of Kanu 2,
There are scores of bamboo crosses in the mud.
There'll be broken hearted women when this tale gets through,
may the living God avenge with yellow blood."

As the year advanced through the early months the activities at the theatre became more and more ambitious. With so many entertainers now available and numerous different groups wanting to produce their own shows, it was necessary to form a management committee. This consisted of the camp commanding officer plus the quartermaster and representatives of the performers, one of whom was our previous concert organizer Eddie Edwins. Appointing a stage manager, scenery designer, publicity manager and a number of general stage hands, regular shows became a weekly fea-

My sketch of the 'Wonder Bar' poster.

The Chungkai Theatre Company and Orchestra in May 1944 after production of Wonder Bar. Leo Britt is far left on stage, Bobby Spong eighth left of back row and Eddie Edwins can also be seen fourth from right giving the 'V' for victory sign in defiance of the Jap photographer.

A scene from Wonder Bar.

ture with performances taking place on Friday and Saturday evenings.

Corporal Leo Britt was an extrovert professional, with experience in films and on the London stage, and he put on the first production which was a very successful revue. We had a preview in Amoebia Hall, due to those well used bamboo thickets being the rehearsal area. Leo was a tough director, bullying the whole cast regardless of rank, but he obtained excellent results.

Fizzer Pearson, who had given us so much enjoyment in the shows at Changi, had also reappeared and formed his own company offering one act plays commencing with 'The Boy Comes Home', followed next by 'The Dear Departed' and then 'The Playgoers'. Bobby Spong joined him to play the female lead with Fizzer taking the role of the leading man.

The publicity manager located a number of artists who painted bill posters advertising each forthcoming attraction, which were displayed on trees around the camp. The same experts made similar posters for the medical officers in anti-fly campaigns, depicting these dangerous pests with the running theme 'The Fly is your Biggest Enemy, Keep it Down'.

Leo and his company went from strength to strength with more ambitious shows, the highlight being the popular London musical 'Wonder Bar'. Performed during the evenings of May 20th and 21st, there was no doubt that it reached new heights; I for one found it difficult to believe that I was watching a show in a prisoner of war camp so far from civilization. Remembered and rewritten by a young officer named John Beckett, with some original songs by Norman Smith, it was performed by a cast of seventeen accompanied by the ten piece band. Among those taking part were Eddie Edwins, Bobby Spong, Eddie Monkhouse and Doc Clark, plus newcomers Gus Harfrey *(formerly a pianist in Sidney Lipton's broadcasting band at the London Grosvenor House Hotel)* and John Wallace. There was a show stopping rendering of 'My Friend Elizabeth' by the latter and Bobby, which they sang and danced to with much panache; for an encore they performed it in French and German. Unfortunately we were deprived of the services of Norman when he was sent to Tamarkan to rejoin No.4 Group, but Ernest Lenthal stepped in as an admirable deputy band leader. With him also went Fizzer, whose final Chungkai presentation had been in April when he had given us Somerset Maugham's 'The Circle'.

Leo though had competition. As well as the Dutch, who were not to be undone, putting their own shows once every six weeks featuring Javanese Eurasians performing traditional native dances, there was Dudley Gotla. He was a doctor with definite views on the type of entertainment that was needed and had long argued with the theatre committee to allow him to put on a knockabout show poking fun of our hosts and the general living conditions. Authorization was finally given for his particular group to go ahead and the end result was the most hilarious performance of them all. It was called 'Thai Diddle Diddle'. Two performances were planned the week after 'Wonder bar', on the 27th and 28th May, but due to rapid developments only the Friday evening show took place. I had booked a seat for this first performance and I was glad that I did, it was too good to have missed.

The dialogue was so audaciously funny, much of it couched in smatterings of Japanese, Malay and pidgin English *(the normal method of communication with our captors).*

The opening sketch portrayed the return home of a British P.O.W. to find an American soldier billeted at his house, whereupon his wife introduces him to his youngest child all of one year old! Not having adjusted himself to normal life he then made his excuses to go to benjo *(toilet)* and as he departs plucks some leaves from a house plant for toilet paper *(it was our custom to use the leaves from surrounding trees and bushes).* Later on he remarks that he would like a pisang *(banana)*, which completely baffles the wife as she misunderstands and hands him an empty fruit bowl. Then followed a lengthy explanation that he had already been to the toilet and that he wanted to eat a banana.

Throughout the show there were many references to "Oromen no goodkana" and "Oromen No.10", even the odd "Kurrah Buggairo", and the watching Japs were obviously becoming restive. Their attitude turned to agitation during the next episode, when three of the lads came on depicting a Wild West scene based on an old cowboy film but dressed in 'Jap-Happies'. Again much Jap-baiting took place and the full company sang a number of parodies, including those we had sung in our huts such as 'The muddy, bloody banks of Kanburi' and 'Once I built a railroad to Bangkok, made it race against time'. Although it was a great morale booster for the audience, the event closed the theatre, the Japs banning all future performances. Dudley thus had a short career as a producer and went back up country within a few weeks as doctor to a 300 strong railway maintenance working party.

There was now a lot of movement as the break up of the Chungkai community began. Initially the demand was for some men to return to the railway working camps to repair damage being inflicted by Allied bombing raids. At first spasmodic, by the end of the year the raids were continuous and from then on until the end of the war the railway was virtually kept out of action. Reconnaissance planes flying at very considerable heights were now frequent, with the Korean guards getting increasingly twitchy at what they called "Come look see, go back speako planes".

Another activity which helped to allay the boredom were the hut lectures. With such a large cross section of people from all walks of life, we had the privilege to listen to many very interesting talks. Who by and where a particular lecture was being given was learned by word of mouth and I think the very first I heard was a well advertised one by Dr. Markovitch. His subject was *"What makes a hormone?"*, which was educationally very interesting to all who attended, even though some came thinking it would be some light hearted fun about 'moaning whores'.

Bob Skene gave us an insight to life as an international polo player who had represented England in the famous prewar Westchester Cup matches against the U.S.A., being especially amusing in his account of socializing with certain film stars on a visit with the team to Hollywood. Captain Ritchie talked of playing tennis at Wimbledon, whilst Lt. Col. Hill, who had been captain of the Worcestershire County Cricket team throughout the twenties, spoke at length on English county cricket. Judge-Advocat Lovel, for whom I had briefly laundered at Selarang, outlined some unusual trials he had presided over in the Siamese courts and Captain Aylwin, a Royal Marine survivor from the sunken Prince of Wales battleship, described the downfall of the German battle-cruiser Bismark. Every night there was someone doing the rounds as a circuit evolved with an endless list of colourful characters talking away. Professional sportsmen, barristers, bridge building engineers from India and regular soldiers all made their contributions, one of the latter being a first world war veteran who had been captured by the Turks at Kut. The treatment meted out there was as horrific as our own and this luckless man was enduring a second dose in his fifties. An even more strange encounter was that told by an officer from the Northumberland Fusiliers. He had been captured in France during 1940 by the Germans but managed to escape prior to being transported to a prisoner of war camp, spending the next twelve months roaming the country as he gradually made his way into the Vichy territory and thence to Marseilles. Picked up once again before reaching there, he again escaped by joining forces with three Scotsmen who bemused the Germans by insisting on speaking in Gaelic only. The underground movement managed to take them across to North Africa from where they boarded ship for Gibralter, arriving home towards the end of 1941. Upon reporting back for duty he found his battalion preparing to leave eastward bound with the 18th Division and he landed with them in Singapore just a few days before capitulation.

There had been a number of well stocked libraries at Changi and the opportunity was taken for some of the books to be brought up with us to Thailand, most men including at least one in their kit. These had subsequently been handed in to the camp administration and were the basis of a reasonable library where reading matter could be borrowed. This gave me the opportunity to read three of Edward Marsh's volumes on the lives and cases of eminent Victorian Counsels, first Sir Edward Marshall-Hall, then Sir Edward Clarke and finally Sir Edward Carson. All four volumes of Compton Mackenzie's "Four Winds of Love" were there, Taylor Caldwell's "Dynasty of Death" and most of A.J. Cronin and Somerset Maugham's novels.

The many books were also the source of titles for the increasingly popular charades. Various huts formed teams who competed in a series of competitions, in fact a number of leagues came into existence, and as standards began to rise some of my friends and I were given the task of finding the most obscure, complex titles possible. I was recruited for this task in conjunction with my duties as one of the librarians. There is no doubt that we had pre-empted television's 'Give us a Clue' by a good many years.

During this period there was also the opportunity for chess and bridge. Some people had brought sets and cards with them, others made them up from all manner of bits and pieces. Lance Bombadier Oppenheim was an expert chess player and often took on six men at a time, invariably beating all of them. When not playing in a match 'Oppy' practised for hours on end on a small card pocket set. He was no ordinary other rank soldier, having enlisted in the Straits Volunteers from his position as professor of mathematics at Raffles University. In the early days he had acted as the Dean of the short lived Changi University, where one could study a large range of subjects, and after the war became a very eminent academician. For several years Chancellor of Malay University, he has been honoured by both Malaysia and Britain and is now the eighty plus year-old Tan Sri Sir Alexander Oppenheim, O.B.E.

Soon after the 'Thai Diddle Diddle' episode, the annual floods overtook us. As in previous years, the water rose from two sources and within a few days the only dry part was on high ground in the central area. Large crowds now trampled about in the confined space, much to the concern of some gardening officers who were growing maize from which they cropped some excellent corn-on-the-cob. During 1943 a few papaya trees had been planted there as well and were now showing signs of bearing fruit. They had no need to be nervous, though, everybody was too food conscious to cause any damage. Incidentally this was not the garden I had worked on for the Japs, that had been outside the camp beyond the cemetery. With the stage under three feet of water and the amphitheatre at least ten, the closure of the theatre became purely academic and in fact now that the river had become a dangerous, roaring torrent, we utilized the area for bathing.

In June a rumour circulated which at first we had difficulty in believing. There were, the story went, Red Cross parcels in the camp awaiting distribution and it was only when the guards were seen smoking American Camel and Chesterfield cigarettes that we gave it credence. Several days later the Japs confirmed that a supply had been received, but when the parcels were eventually issued we found they had been considerably plundered. Although each one was clearly marked "American Red Cross, one parcel per man", we had to make do in sharing one between six, the remainder having obviously been purloined. None the less everybody was very excited at the long forgotten luxuries, even if each group of six had to draw lots for a share of the contents, such as powdered milk, chocolate, scented soap, real cigarettes, cocoa, razor blades and various tinned foods. I was a little disappointed not to sample the foodstuffs, my straw giving me the soap. Still, it was a joy to lather up and it lasted for quite a long while. The brand name was Swan and to ensure not losing it in the river after the floods had subsided, I bored a hole through for attachment to my neck with a piece of atap tie that was normally used for lashing the bamboo slats together. These were the first and last Red Cross parcels to reach us.

That year we experienced the usual seasonal electric storms, but the local rainfall was not so severe and the high river waters were due to persistent wet weather in the northern region. The floods subsided in July when we witnessed a rare phenomenon, a total eclipse of the sun. As the day turned suddenly into night I filled my haversack with water to look at the reflection, the doctors having warned everyone not to gaze directly at the sun under any circumstances. I understand that this was a most infrequent event, it having only happened once more, fairly recently, since 1944.

Although many men continued to die, the sterling work of the dedicated doctors and their tireless helpers gradually brought an improvement in the condition of a large number of the sick who had come down from the working camps with broken bodies. Amputations went on for the chronic ulcer cases, eventually reaching a total of 240 that survived. A remedial centre was established where they, plus others who had lost the use of their limbs due to beriberi and also ulcer patients who had escaped the knife, were able to do some simple exercises under supervision.

The fitter amongst us even ventured at this stage into a little football and rugby. Bamboo goalposts went up on the open areas between our hut and the hospital, whilst balls miraculously appeared. Soon there had to be a match between England and Scotland, in which that gifted singing doctor, James Clark, played for the latter. He was, apparently, a Scottish Junior International. Another doctor, Major Black, turned out in one of the rugby matches and was roundly cheered as he scored a try by diving headlong on the slithering surface of the pitch, the game having been played in pouring rain. Major C'On Wallis, M.C. of the East Surreys organized the matches, but could not play due to being laid low with the 200 or so in Amoebia Hall, which was a pity as he happened to be an Irish International player and his skills would have added to the entertainment. The Major had won his Military Cross in action as adjutant with the British Battalion in Singapore.

The sight of Allied planes passing overhead was by now almost a daily event and reports came down the line of regular air raids on the Burma section. It was only a matter of time, we felt, before some of the more strategically located camps were hit and in due course news came through that there had been an attack on

Thanbyuzayat. A number of casualties were sustained by P.O.Ws, but after a second raid the camp was thankfully evacuated. Travelling on the railway was now a dangerous matter, with journeys taking a very long time as the drivers were constantly stopping and starting in an effort to remain inconspicuous. Unfortunately one train carrying prisoners was hit, killing thirteen of our men and wounding many others. Obviously the railway had become a prime target.

With the railway construction having been completed several months beforehand, the Japs now began to find other uses for their large labour force. All of the fittest men had been segregated in the northern part of the camp and formed into groups of 150 strong, prior to leaving for Singapore en route for Japan. There they would be worked in coal mines and steelworks, although this was not known at the time and most of the men looked upon it as an improvement on life in Thailand with its tragic memories. They were issued with some warm clothing, it being a mixture of British Army Hospital Blues, kilts and both Dutch and British serge uniforms taken from captured stores left behind in depots in Malaya and Indonesia. Each group were a motley collection but at least it was SOMETHING to wear, which nobody had previously received. Everybody left in high spirits, but sadly very few were to reach their destination.

Following the long weary train journey back to Singapore, they boarded an ancient vessel immediately. Crammed into holds which were at once battened down, they commenced the perilous sea voyage in appalling conditions which worsened with each passing day. It was off the coast of the Phillipine Islands that they met their doom, when the convoy was attacked by American destroyers. Being completely unaware of the cargo, the raiders sank every ship resulting in the majority of the passengers drowning; when they realized who the men in the sea were, the destroyers delayed their departure and picked up some survivors. The lucky few arrived back in Britain in September 1944, bringing with them the first news of our treatment in Thailand and elsewhere since the fall of Singapore, which shocked and horrified the whole civilized world. Among the casualties were several East Surreys, including Company Sergeant Major Shemmings who had managed the Sandilands Rest Camp in Penang. Bobby Spong, that marvellous entertainer, was another. Not originally selected to go, he had pleaded to join some of his friends who were included in the party; he had amused and given enjoyment to so many and was to be greatly missed.

Next came the time for some of the sick to move on. A special camp to cater for all groups was being set up at Nakhon Pathom, which was a sizeable town away from the rivers, fifty miles distant beyond Banpong and about halfway to Bangkok. So it was decided to transfer the amoebic cases there, but I did not accompany them.

CHAPTER 14.

NAKHON PATHOM.

At the end of April, Doctor Black had transferred me from the amoebic section into a general medical ward. He considered this necessary due to my deteriorating condition, general debility having brought on tachycardia - a rapid heartbeat condition. Its constant thump, thump, thump was relentlessly disturbing and when I began to experience chest pains he dug into his drug reserves and treated me with a course of digitalis injections. This helped with the pains, but the pulsations never really left me completely and in fact I have never fully recovered. At no time since was I able to run, whilst climbing any gradients has always been difficult.

So I was separated from my friendly companions of the past eight months and, with the exodus of so many people, there was an air of emptiness about Chungkai. However for those who remained there was the bonus of the theatre reopening, the floods having subsided and the Japanese ban lifted. Great ones for collective punishment, they now considered that we had been taught a lesson for our insolence.

Leo had lost quite a lot of his performers, some going on the Japan parties, others to Tamarkan or Nakhon Pathom. It was now the time to switch his talents to producing straight plays, the first presentation being Emlyn Williams 'Night Must Fall' with a cast of nine players. The baritone who had sung to us with Eddie's earlier troupe, Colonel Outram, and Hugh de Wardener both appeared in this play. The latter was a pleasant, red headed doctor who was one of the few left remaining from 'Wonder Bar', having fitted in his acting with a busy life in the hospital. During the cholera epidemic he had given heroic service, for which an M.B.E. was subsequently awarded; in later life Hugh became an eminent Professor of Medicine in London. The show was another great success for Leo, even though the second evening's performance was stopped halfway through due to heavy rainfall. This was the start of severe late season rains that precipitated second floodings that year, according to the Thais a most unusual occurrence.

Towards the end of August it was time for the rest of the 'heavy sick' to leave for Nakhon Pathom. We assembled by the camp gates, where everybody was subjected to a rigorous search by the jittery Japs. For some time past snap searches at any time of the day or night had become commonplace and the possession of any writing materials strictly forbidden. Furthermore only the barbers were allowed to retain any razors or knives and even they had to be handed in to the Jap guardhouse every day at 4pm and drawn out again the next morning. The search completed we moved off for the station to board our train, but not until going through the ritual of yet another search. Unfortunately on the day of departure I was suffering from an attack of dengue fever and running a high temperature, making it necessary for me to be stretchered out to the train, where we climbed aboard open sided trucks which were pulled by a lumbering old wood burning steam engine. I felt most relieved to be outside the confines of the camp where, except for the brief forays on bamboo gathering parties, we had been incarcerated for over a year and could quite understand the almost jubilant feelings of the departed Japan drafts. Upon reaching Tamarkan it was not possible to be anything but impressed by the two bridges that had been built across the river. At the point where we had crossed over by barge on our way to Wun Lun, the first one to be erected was of wooden construction, whilst alongside it had followed a more permanent building with concrete pillars and steel girders. It was now receiving regular attention by Allied bombers and was so badly damaged by the end of 1944 that movement of Jap troops and materials was seriously curtailed. Our men in the nearby Tamarkan and Kanburi camps had the exasperating task of carrying out repairs after every air raid.

Nowadays the bridge is still in regular use, serving the initial 100 kilometres of the railway up to Hintok - the remainder has long since been reclaimed by the jungle - and is now commercially exploited by the tourist trade as "The Bridge on the River Kwai". The bridge in that particular film was fictional and it existed only in the author's imagination.

Nakhon Pathom is dominated by the tallest stupa in Thailand which, rising to 380 feet, is one of the most important in the whole Buddhist faith. Restored in the mid-nineteenth century by King Mongkut *(on whom the King of Siam in the musical "The King and I" was based)*, it is known as the Pra Pathom Chedi and is bell shaped with its huge dome being covered all over with gold coloured tiles. The impact when reflected in the brilliant sunshine was a sight to behold.

Buddhist stupa at Nakhon Pathom, the 380 feet high Phra Pathom Chedi.

Alighting from the train at the station in the shadow of this magnificent building, we were promptly marched away without any more of the delays usually experienced when travelling anywhere under the Japs. The ride and open surroundings had had a beneficial effect on me and, my fever having eased, I was able to march with the others as we proceeded through the streets of the town. Upon passing over a level crossing we halted at the camp gates, to be faced with another detailed search and it was only after the guards eventual satisfaction that we were allowed to enter. That though was not the end of the interrogations, once inside the same routine took place; what they thought we could have acquired on the journey puzzled me. No doubt they were hunting for clues leading to the whereabouts of secret radios, in addition to the normal contraband such as writing materials which indicated their desire to prevent diaries being compiled.

We found ourselves in a well laid out camp, with rows of huts with wooden frames, rattan walls and roofs of atap. They were bigger than the bamboo jungle ones and this was a definite improvement for we taller people. The sleeping platforms were better, being made from wooden planks instead of bamboo slats, and the latrines, which were located between each hut, had covered in access. This meant reaching them at night in the rain was not so hazardous and the provision of a trap door meant they could be regularly emptied by sanitation parties for disposal in a cesspool pit. Even so, due to the many flies, the surrounding paths were continuously crawling with fat white maggots.

Len was here and so we joined forces once more with most of the other lads from Amoebia Hall, although 'Happy' Allen had been transferred to the tuberculosis ward following a relapse of the disease he had contracted in the early days. Jack Griffin was also here and so was Red Jennings, an extrovert Scotsman who had written permission to sport a magnificent red, bushy beard. From the very start of our captivity military discipline had, whenever the conditions allowed, been maintained to boost morale and in line with army tradition the wearing of beards was frowned upon. Red had decided to grow his immediately he was captured and vowed to keep it until release, so, being a loyal Argyll, took the precaution of obtaining a note from his commanding officer.

Among the other men in our hut were a number of Australians, Dutch and Americans, this being the first occasion when the different nationalities were not segregated. There were only a few Americans in Thailand, some of them sailor survivors from the USS Houston sunk in the battle of the Java Seas in 1942 and the others soldiers of a Texan National Guard field artillery battery. These gunners had, like the 18th Division at Singapore, been hastily sent to Dutch East Indies shortly before the fall of Java. I soon made friends with a number of them, particularly Harvey Boatman from Houston, Texas with his fascinating, lazy southern drawl, Aussies Jack Applecamp from Alice Springs right in the centre of the Australian continent and Ted Gould who was a Queenslander from Brisbane, and a Dutchman born and bred in Batavia *(now Jakarta)*, Piet Ouborg.

Yanagida had come from Chungkai to command the Nakhon Pathom area, but we saw very little of him. It being basically a hospital camp, the doctors were in charge under the direction of Lieut.

Col. Coats who was another very fine surgeon. A man then already some fifty years of age he too, like his compatriot Weary Dunlop, was to be honoured in due course with a knighthood and the O.B.E. The latter had also come down from Chungkai and these two, assisted by the other Australian, British and Dutch doctors, were to perform over one thousand operations in the camp within the next year. They tackled complex brain and complicated abdominal surgery, including colostomies and ileostomies and, such was the skill of these devoted men, the mortality rate here was kept down to just two and a half per cent. It must always be remembered that this work was done with limited facilities and restricted availability of drugs.

Operating theatre.

At the dentist's surgery.

Medical inspection room.

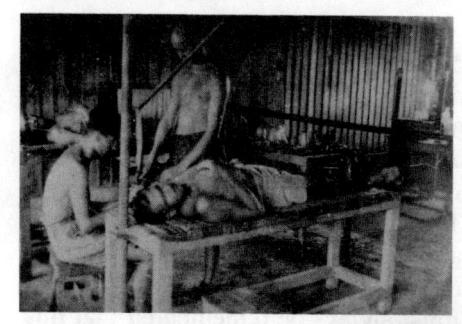

A blood transfusion in progress.

The pathological laboratory.

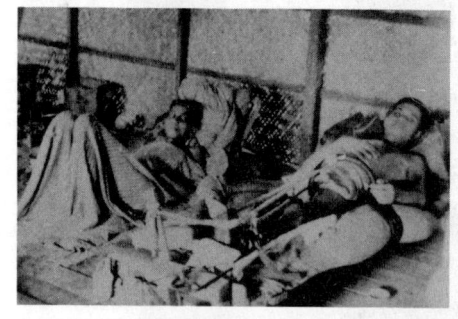

Dutch/Javanese surgical patient in 'heavy' sick hut.

Major Fisher, an Australian physician from Sydney, was the consultant in our section and our day to day doctor Captain Street, the Beds and Herts medical officer. These two hard working men gave each of the new intake a thorough examination and kept us all under close supervision, prescribing me an egg a day for one month to counteract the debility and the reappearance of pellagra on the insteps of my feet. About a couple of weeks later, however, I went down with what I thought was another bout of dengue fever, running a temperature of 104 degrees. During the next few days I was in a state of semi-coma, having little idea of my surroundings; no food passed my lips and I had vague recollections of someone forcing quinine powder into my mouth. In due course the medicine did its work and I came to with an anxious Len peering down at me. This was no dengue but a return of the malaria that had escaped me for the past eighteen months.

It was several weeks before I was well enough to visit the washing shed near a pond that had been dug to provide a water supply, my companions bringing me back enough water to keep me reasonably clean during this period. I was glad to be eating again, even though the rations were even more restricted because all of the inhabitants were sick and only entitled to half the normal rice allowance. Two ounces of meat per man per day was still the issue, although occasionally this was substituted by fish which we devoured with relish - heads and tails included.

The very extensive camp held about 7000 'patients' and was encircled by an earth bund ten feet high and wide, which kept us well hidden from the local population. The guards patrolled along its top, as well as continuing inside where they subjected us to sudden searches any time of the day or night. Tenkos were usually conducted within the huts, everyone having to stand by their bedspace and number in Japanese as the guard passed through. On some days the procedure was changed when we paraded outside and in our absence the huts would be raided in yet more of the interminable searches. There was a canteen of sorts, for people still in a position to raise any cash, but it was in no way as big as the PRI had been in Chungkai. Eggs cooked in a variety of ways, sambals and fruit such as limes, pomeloes and bananas were available; a fried egg on a five cent bread was a particular favourite.

We had come to accept the regular passage of Allied planes as normal, but on one moonlight night in September, I was awakened by the drone of aircraft and found everyone pouring outside to watch the sky. It was obvious that a large raid was taking place in the vicinity, we could hear the crumph, crumph of exploding bombs reverberating like thunder and the heavens were festooned with bright orange lights. We cheered our heads off, completely unmolested by either the Japs or Koreans who had taken cover in their newly dug slit-trenches. Our joy was not to last long, as news reached us the next morning that the target had been Nonpladuk, which was less than ten miles away between Nakhon Pathom and Banpong. There the POW camp had been established adjacent to the marshalling yards on the main Singapore to Bangkok railway but, despite pleas stressing its dangers, evacuation had been steadfastly refused. The yards had been the official target and the first foray was completely successful, destroying engines and rolling stock, but unfortunately disaster struck with the second wave. Bombs fell directly on the camp resulting in an awful carnage, with casualties of 100 dead and 400 wounded; a Dutch party that had arrived in the camp only the previous day had been housed in temporary accommodation at the nearest point to the railway and incurred the heaviest death rate. It was the unkindest cut of all.

A day or so later some daylight leaflet raids took place and a number of messages were soon circulating, even though picking them up or retaining possession was threatened with dire consequences. The texts contained encouraging news, gave a precis of the war's progress to date and stated *"Don't worry lads, it won't be long now - Big Bill Slim is coming to get you out"*. Who the heck we conjectured was Big Bill Slim?

Nakmon Pathom did not possess a theatre, the one at Chungkai having been somewhat unique, but a rough earthen open stage had been built on which occasional concerts were given. Some of the artistes had come with us but most of the performers were newcomers, one of them being one of my new friends, Jack Applecamp. He was a professional ventriloquist and had faithfully hung on to his dummy through thick and thin; as well as putting on his turns, Jack was not adverse to throwing his voice during tenko with an extra number. This would cause some confusion to the counting Jap who found that the hut population had suddenly increased! Adept also at the deaf and dumb language, he instructed us in the art so that we could converse, and make fun of the guard, during the ritual when complete silence was ordered.

The hut lectures were resumed. Sergeant Len Muncer of the Sherwood Foresters talked of his experiences as a county cricketer with Middlesex at Lords and lawyer Eric Griffiths-Jones was most entertaining with stories at the bar. Also touring the huts regularly were itinerant singers, musicians and comics entertaining the many sick who were too ill to attend the organized shows. One of these performers spoke with a pronounced lisp, but this did not dissuade him from a funny routine of stand up jokes; he also sang well, the song "Look for a Silver Lining" being his speciality

Despite all of the unheralded searches, plus lightning raids by the infamous Kempati, the secret radio continued to operate. So the news was circulated verbally on a regular basis, Captain Back, yet another lawyer, now being our newscaster. It was he who kept us up to date with the American recapture of the Phillipine Islands, illustrating their advances by drawing diagrams in the dirt on the ground. His intimate knowledge of Mindano and Leyte enabled him to outline them from memory with remarkable clarity.

Fizzer Pearson and Norman Smith were among us once more and as the third Christmas of our captivity approached arrangements commenced to produce a special show for the occasion. Norman located a few of his old band to provide the music, whilst our entertaining lawyer, Eric Griffith-Jones plus Major E.W. Swanton and a number of others were co-opted to take part. The show was a spoof on the Aladdin pantomime called 'Alf's Magic Ring', the highlights being a very funny double act by Fizzer and Griffith-Jones, as well as Swanton playing the part of the genie by using his broadcasting voice backstage projected through a dummy wireless set. There was much good natured banter in the script, directed at the many Australians in the audience. In one sketch Fizzer and his partner were depicted flying on a magic carpet and as they gazed down from above one of them remarked that he could see a strange object below which he thought looked like some old pieces of bamboo. His companion then made a careful study of it and concluded that of course it was obviously Sydney Harbour Bridge. The outcome was a torrent of catcalls from the Aussies and cheers from the British, the former revering this structure as virtually a seventh wonder of the world.

A parody of an old music hall song called "Any dirty work to do" was sang by this inimitable pair with the refrain "For two fried eggs and a five cent bread, we'll teach you how to swing the lead and convince the doctor that you're half dead, any dirty work to do". The inference was that it was possible to bribe the medics on the many medical parades that were now taking place to select working parties for numerous new projects in different areas of Thailand, the said delicacy being available at the canteen. The concert concluded with the singing of the National Anthem and I went back to my hut hoping against hope that his surely must be our last Christmas away from home and our loved ones.

Captain Griffith-Jones settled in Kenya after the war and in due course was Chairman of the Guthrie Corporation, the largest trading organization in Africa. He also served as Attorney-General in the Kenyan government, in which post he received a knighthood.

On New Year's Day, 1945 a new diversion took place, when we had the pleasure of witnessing a special 'cricket' match. For some time past Major Swanton and a group of fellow enthusiasts had been playing a form of knock-about cricket between the huts, which took place during the short period separating the evening meal and tenko. This activity soon attracted the attention of the Aussies and now a Test Match had been arranged between England and their old sporting foe. The pitch was an area some eighty feet wide, faced by huts either side, and one hundred and sixty in length so, due to lack of space, there was just one wicket comprising five bamboo stumps at the batsman's crease and only one at the bowler's end. The strange conditions precluded the normal method of running between the wickets, all of the scores counting as boundaries once the batsman had steered the ball past the eight fieldsmen. The long huts that extended along the pitch on each border were flanked with a drainage trench running alongside and it counted as one run for hits into the ditch and two over the hut. Fours and sixes applied when the ball was hit past the bowler, behind whom there were rows of trees backing onto the surrounding camp bund; woebetide anyone who sent it over the top, the balls were extremely precious. A tennis ball had to suffice, which was constantly soaked in a tin of water placed near the bowler's wicket *(this gave it added weight)*, and the bat was hewn from an ordinary piece of planking.

Several hundred spectators squatted on the ground under the shade of the large clump of trees immediately behind the batsman and the game started, with England batting first. The team was captained by Major Swanton and our two old theatrical friends Norman and Fizzer were also playing, displaying yet further talents. Runs came fast and furious, notwithstanding much raucous barracking, in the manner of the famous Sydney Hill, by the Australian spectators and the innings was eventually declared closed. When the Aussies came in to bat they faced a demon bowler, none other than Fizzer who was no mean cricketer, having represented Lincolnshire in the Minor Counties competition. There was an immediate sensation when he arrived at the wicket prepared to bowl. The rest of the players were bare footed on the hot sun baked soil but Fizzer was actually wearing boots and this appeared to have a devastating effect on the opposition. Wickets fell rapidly with our star performer hitting the stumps time and time again, even the captain, everyone's hero Weary Dunlop, failed to stem the flow. He had strode to the wicket to resounding cheers from his supporters and cries of "Good on yer, Weary, give the Poms a go", but it was not to be as his wicket was quickly spread-eagled. Its fall signalled the end of the match and we all trooped back for tenko in a good humour that was equally shared by the British and Australians alike. The few Dutchmen, too, who had come along had thoroughly enjoyed themselves, despite being completely puzzled by the ritual.

Len was on the move again. He had attended one of those medical parades and had been considered fit enough to join a working party going to Ratburi some thirty miles away. So on yet one more occasion we bade each other farewell, not to meet again until I had returned home when it was all over. I did hear from him a couple of months after his departure, when I received a note via a returning sick party. It was written on the back of one of the twenty-five word letters that had come from the girlfriend whom he believed had deserted him and said:

"Dear Jack,

Just a few lines to let you know that I am still alive and kicking. I have been quite fit since leaving N.K. and have been working every day down here. You will be interested to know that I am "mucking in" with Arther Leatherland who has turned up from Burma - he got caught at Sumatra. I have actually received as many as thirty letters in this camp, including the one I am writing on. I have sent you this one especially to show you that I am caught hook, line and sinker. What do you think of it? No more bachelor days for me if she has her own way. Remember me to all the boys down there, Happy Allen, Tom Clough, Roderick and the rest. Tell them the SAD news about the female. I hope you are all keeping pretty well and getting plenty of mail. Must ring off now. Hope to be seeing you soon. It won't be long now.

Len"

In February 1945 the Japs changed their policy relating to the officers, deciding that they should now be segregated from the other ranks. All of them, with the exclusion of most of the doctors and padres, moved to their own camp at Kanburi which left the remainder of us in Nakhon Pathom much reduced in numbers. We were sorry to see then go, the majority who were fit enough having helped so tirelessly on general camp fatigues, such as sanitation duties and antimalarial precautions.

It was at this time that I began to experience another problem. One night I felt a certain stiffness about the hips and severe pains whenever I turned, which increased with intensity during the day. Nothing seemed to bring relief and within a few days the mere action of lowering my legs off the sleeping platform on to the ground resulted in the most excruciating pain. It took me a long time to reach a standing position and I became trapped on my bed-space, only leaving it to make the difficult trip to the latrines, my immediate companions Jack Griffin and Harvey Boatman kindly collecting my meals. They even took my turn in the lagi *(more)* queue, which was always formed at meal times to share any left overs once the normal portions had been served. Everyone was allocated a number to make sure that any surplus was fairly shared, thereby preventing the same men from always getting to the head of the queue. Major Fisher gave me a detailed examination after he had been on his rounds and diagnosed osteo-arthritis of the sacroliac joints, telling Captain Street to give me half an aspirin! Naturally it had little effect but at least it was a gesture and I was lucky to get anything at all.

Later on a certain amount of drugs supplied by the Red Cross were allowed into the camp. The largest quantity of medicants were calamine lotion and castor oil, neither of which helped us a lot, especially the latter as we certainly had no need to induce diarrhoea. Limited amounts of the extremely valuable emetine were included and we all reflected on how many lives would have been saved if some had been provided two years earlier. These comments also applied to the anti-diphtheria serums now received. Somewhat surprisingly there was a supply of sodium salicytate which the Major now prescribed me and this treatment had a definitely beneficial effect, bringing a considerable lessening of pain.

Then the malaria attacked again as fiercely as ever and, with the arthritis, tachycardia and amoebic dysentery still plaguing me, it was decided that I should move into a special hut housing the 'heavy sick'. As it was only two rows away it was still possible to keep in touch with my former hut-mates, but I soon made a number of new friends in the new environment. A section at one end was screened off which contained about thirty tuberculosis cases, Happy Allen among them, and I found myself occupying a bed space next door. Most of my companions here were post operative patients, the two immediately adjacent being young Australians who had been given appendectomies by Weary Dunlop; both had been left with a tube protruding through which they received periodic 'washouts'. Terry Thume came from Townsville in the most northerly part of Queensland and Bill Dunne was a Victorian from Melbourne. Some of the others had been subject to even more serious operations, such as colostomies, performed to stop the ravages of chronic dysentery. Norman Hawkins from Braunstone in Leicestershire was one and he, like the rest, had been fitted with a container adapted from the oval shaped Dutch Army water bottle. These were strapped over the exposed bowel with standard army webbing. Also in our bay were Norman Atkinson who was an Anglo-Indian from Lucknow who had received the same operation as the Aussie pair; the middle aged Australian Dick Bartlett suffering from general debility, and finally there was a broad accented Yorkshireman from Keighley, Dodger Green, struggling with asthma.

The senior medical orderly ruled us all with a rod of iron. Tynesider John 'Geordie' Guthrie made the rounds daily to administer the coarse quinine powder to all those currently experiencing an attack of malaria. This was the only version now available and even that was in short supply, so he made up a special measure about the size of a thimble to ensure that there was no wastage. It was unpleasant to the taste, but Geordie made sure that everybody took their correct dosage throughout the ten day course, despite everything eaten having a bitter flavour. At the end of the period I found the treatment was causing dizziness and a remote kind of deafness. The malaria fevers subsided though - until the next time!

Geordie tended the TB incumbents with great devotion, so much so that he developed the disease after returning home. Happily he was soon cured by modern drugs and became well enough to take up hospital nursing in the National Health Service. Jack Griffin also abandoned his old job and went into this profession.

Terry, Bill and I came from completely different backgrounds but we really appreciated each other's company. Terry had spent much of his early youth in the Queensland outback, driving herds of sheep across the state in six week treks, whilst Bill was a suburbanite from Melbourne. The famous billiard and snooker champions Walter and Horace Lindrum were his uncles.

Several of their Australian friends were welcome regular visitors to the hut and one of them, Colin Coles-Smith from Brisbane, used to bring along a backgammon set *(or Acey-Deucy as he called it)*. It was my introduction to a game which provided hours of amusement.

I had been able to preserve a number of photographs of my home and family life and my new Australian companions liked to look at them. When Colin saw a black and white studio portrait of my fiancee he suggested that a Dutchman in his hut might well be able to colour it, so we went off in search of him. The artist quickly agreed and went to work immediately, with a remarkable end result. He had reproduced almost the exact shade of red, based on my description, of her long evening gown. Ted Gould next said that such a work of art should be properly presented and, being a bookbinder by trade, went to work to mount and encase it in a handsome folder. He had scrounged some pieces of card and dark brown paper and glued them up with rice water. Still in my possession, the folder and portrait are in as good condition today as they were when my cosmopolitan friends completed their handiwork. My thanks to both Ted and that unnamed Dutch painter.

Joan's portrait in Ted Gould's folder.

As the Jap forces were driven further down Burma by the 14th Army, more and more working parties were being assembled to build routes through the jungle to facilitate their retreat. In March a group departed for an unknown destination, but it was believed that they went into the Mergui region where the work was to prove every bit as strenuous as that on the railway construction. To make matters worse they were stricken by a mystery fever from which few recovered - the death rate was alarming. 'Polly' Saunders and George Cast, two friends of mine from the East Surreys, lost their lives here. Polly had been my hut mate in Shanghai, the Chinese High School at Bukit Timah and also Tangjong Pau; George was a regular army sergeant who had returned home from Shanghai in early 1939 and then came back in charge of a small draft of militia men who had followed us out in 1940. Both were quite well and in high spirits upon leaving Nakhon Pathom.

So remotely had the survivors of this final savagery penetrated the jungle that at the end of hostilities even the Jap Command HQ in Bangkok did not know where they were and it took an advance party of the British Special Services three weeks to locate them.

With the departure of the newly impressed working parties, those remaining were contained in a much smaller area. The vacated sections became occupied by Japanese troops and a bund was built surrounding us, indicating a possible change in our fortunes. These were further enhanced one afternoon by a spectacular event that convinced everyone that the end of our imprisonment was near. At the time I had gone across to the furthermost point of the camp where the shaving point was located, George Greaves having long since parted company with me, and was being shaved by an Australian barber. He had just completed one side of my face when suddenly there was a roar of diving, firing planes. Rushing outside we witnessed a stimulating spectacle of fighter aircraft screaming down in a surprise attack on a small grass aerodrome a mile or so down the road, where a number of old by-planes were based. The raid convinced us all that the use of fighters must mean that our armies were near and some even believed that a force must have landed. It was of course pure optimism, the raiders having flown in from aircraft carriers, so our joy was short lived and we still had a few months to endure before relief was to come. Nevertheless we all returned to our normal routine greatly heartened - I never did get the rest of that shave.

Malaria had by now taken a severe hold on me, returning repeatedly as a monthly occurrence. The quinine treatment only seemed to keep the attacks at bay for about three weeks and the resulting rigors, fevers, enlarged spleen and the side effects of the medicine combined to make me feel more debilitated than ever. Yet another outbreak of the osteo-arthritis added to my discomfort and without the comradeship of my newly found friends things would have been much worse to bear. Fellowship was the one redeeming feature of those difficult days.

I liked the Australians, they were SO resilient. There was always much good humoured banter about the Poms, as they called the British, and the 'transplanted Poms' when referring to prewar immigrants in their own ranks. Despite the outward tough image, though, many Aussies were attracted to the arts with a special affinity to poetry. The world renowned Australian poet Banjo Paterson was a national hero and Terry in particular was a great fan of Rudyard Kipling. Upon learning that I lived in a town beside the River Thames he immediately sat down beside me and quoted the following extract from "The River's Tale":

> *"And life was gay and the world was new*
> *and I was a mile across at Kew,*
> *But the Romans came with a heavy hand*
> *and bridged and roaded and ruled the land.*
> *Then the Romans left and the Danes blew in*
> *and that's where your history books begin."*

CHAPTER 15.

IT'S ALL OVER.

News of the end of hostilities in Europe was confirmed by Boon Pong. This gentleman was a Thai entrepreneur in Kanburi who was the main contractor for the supply of rations and it was from him that the canteen management obtained their goods. He had been of invaluable help to us during the long captivity in his country, using his delivery service to smuggle into the camps medical supplies made available by both the Swiss and Swedish Consulates. In addition to this, large sums of money were advanced personally against I.O.Us, for repayment after the war, which allowed the purchase of extra foodstuffs; he also accepted valuables from men who did not wish to part with them against cash for eventual redemption. These transactions were conducted by the various camp 'racketeers' and the debts were all gratefully repaid in the fullness of time.

It was subsequently learned that Boon had been senior officer in the Thai underground movement and, albeit only after lengthy lobbying by several of our commanding officers, he was decorated by the British Government.

I continued on the malarial seesaw over the next few months and August arrived with me yet once again taking the daily spoonful of quinine. We had already learned that Rangoon had fallen to General Slim's advancing troops and the air was full of rumours. For some while there had been a change in the attitude of the normally sullen Korean guards, who were now no longer conspicuous within the camp boundaries and just keeping to patrolling along the top of the surrounding bund. During the night of the 15th, they seemed to have disappeared altogether and with startling and exciting stories abounding nobody slept much, groups of people chatting away animatedly throughout the small hours. Piet Ouborg was convinced that it was all over and came across to shake me warmly by the hand, but I was not so confident and steadfastly refused to agree until I was sure. I was wrong. In the morning it was obvious that something was afoot and when Yanagida summoned Colonel Coats to his office all doubts evaporated.

He was informed that there had been a pronouncement by the Emperor stating that Japan had surrendered to the Allied Forces and we learned early in the afternoon that we were free men. After such a long isolation it was difficult to appreciate the wonderful news and, not unnaturally, everybody was in an exceptionally buoyant mood. There was much hand shaking and back slapping and soon all those who were mobile migrated to the earthen stage in the central area, where an impromptu singsong quickly got under way. We were a happy collection of Britons, Australians, Americans and Dutch and I think it is true to say that all and everyone of us had but one initial thought, I'VE MADE IT.

Colonel Coats immediately took over full control, instructing the Japanese and Koreans to remain contained within the confines of their own quarters. Arrangements were made for an improvement in the rations, increasing the issue of rice, meat and vegetables as much as possible; supplies of course were limited but a whole pomelo apiece each day was definite bonus. Over the next few days more detailed news came through of the momentous events and we were mystified by talk of a huge new weapon, called an atomic bomb, that had devastated Hiroshima and Nagasaki. Completely unaware of its portent, we were extremely thankful that the raids had been instrumental in bringing the war to an earlier close and thereby advancing our release. This was particularly apt in view of developments of which we were all blissfully unaware.

With the plan for a British invasion force to land simultaneously in Malaya and the coast in the Gulf of Siam on the 18th of August *(they were already at sea when the surrender was announced)*, standing instructions had been issued by the Imperial Japanese Army Commander-in-Chief to massacre all of the prisoners of war in the area when the enemy landed. Lord Mountbatten suspected that such a policy might be implemented and had arranged for the Air Force to drop arms into all known POW camps for our own self defence. When these facts came to light at home the following year I chillingly realized the motive behind the encirclement within the bunds, from which the crossfire would have decimated us.

All of us, regardless of nationality, were astounded by the unbelievable news that there had been a change of government in

Britain. How could they have held a General Election when so many thousands of us were deprived of the vote? My friends among the Australians and Americans were even more incredulous, Harvey Boatman exclaiming: "But Churchill *is* Britain, he won the war and you just cannot cast him aside."

I tried to explain the intricacies of British politics, but to no avail as he wandered away solemnly shaking his head. It was to be the first indication of the general attitude in Britain to the Far Eastern half of the war; the soubriquet "The Forgotten Army" was not without foundation.

For the next few days we wondered what the first development would be and then our initial visitor from the 'outside' arrived. This was a sergeant from the Special Air Services, carrying a strange looking weapon which he explained was a Sten Gun, who belonged to a detachment of parachutists who had been in the neighbourhood for a couple of months observing our conditions and liaising with the Free Thai Movement. The biggest impression he had on me was his appearance, he seemed to be so big and well covered, and to see someone so fit was a revelation; we had become accustomed to each others feeble condition to such an extent that it had become normal. This man looked so PINK.

The next event was a visit from the Royal Air Force. Having sent messages requesting that the centre of the camp be cleared of all personnel and plainly marked out as drop area, they flew over the following day dropping vital supplies. A flight of planes that we had never seen before, they were Dakotas, circulated above and smartly clad airmen in well ironed khaki drill shirts and shorts could be seen quite clearly at the wide open doors. At first everyone thought they were waving at us, but it was quickly realized that we were being requested to stand clear before parachuted bundles of goodies were released. Soon they were raining down and, although a few missed the target and landed in a damaged condition, the majority reached us safely.

This was a joyous day. There was plenty for all including strange looking jungle green bush-jackets and slacks plus some American Army biscuit coloured shirts and trousers; brown army plimsolls, grey army socks and green berets. I received the American gear and an adequate supply of soap, toothpaste and brush, a razor with shaving soap and finally hair brush and comb. It was all sheer heaven and I must have cleaned my teeth at least a dozen times on the first day, savouring the luscious flavour of my Kolynos toothpaste with relish. It was a popular brand in those days and I even found pleasure in just looking at its distinctive yellow packet. Washing all over with a lush lather in hot water with proper soap was also bliss, in fact everything that is taken for granted in normal day to day life was to be so from now on.

There was also food and medicines aplenty in the drop, which were channelled to the cook-house and medical authorities for fair distribution.

For the present everybody was advised to keep within the camp boundaries, but official parties were arranged to visit the huge Golden Statue of Buddha in the nearby stupa. Unfortunately many, including myself, could not go due to their physical condition making the climb up the large number of steps out of the question.

True to his word, Red Jennings shaved off his voluminous red beard and it altered his appearance so much that when he walked into the hut I almost failed to recognize him. With the adornment he gave one the impression of being a big, dominating man; he now seemed quite small and insignificant. I, too, had shaved off my moustache, no longer to be referred to as 'the sergeant over there with the moustache' when anyone happened to be looking for me. Perhaps I also now presented a different image to my fellows.

The weeks passed and we began to experience some frustration at the continued delay in any developments towards release. It was of course appreciated that repatriation was a tremendous task, the mere location alone of the many camps throughout the whole of Asia being monumental. Groups of men arrived from up country, among them my old friends Wis and Taffy, as their camps began to close down. They were from the more established locations and searches started for others, the Japs not being sure where everybody was - the lost Mergui Road party being a case in point. When these poor unfortunates were eventually discovered they were greatly reduced in numbers, the general conditions and that mystery fever having taken their toll.

Our gallant doctors now had the help of some medical officers who had flown in. Although appalled at the general standard of health they were very impressed with our universal good spirits, having quite expected to find us depressed at best, if not mentally affected by our ordeal. On the second of September one of them was asked, immediately upon arrival, to tell us frankly how we appeared to him. He commented that we looked like, ate like, smelt like and dressed like natives, which was quite apt. Having endured our conditions for so long together, the odd sour smell of the camp had been accepted as normal, as had the general lack of clothing and eating food resembling swill from old tin cans.

With rumours constantly circulating there was a whisper that a visit by none other than Lady Louis Mountbatten was imminent. No one could believe that this could possibly be true because, it was said, she is married to a royal and will be safely back in England; some went even further and commented on her known reputation as a social butterfly, remembering her days as a leader of the Bright Young Things of the nineteen twenties. On Thursday the 6th September 1945 we were in for a surprise. She really did arrive.

When Yanagida learned of this momentous event he had the audacity to position himself at the main gate, ready to greet her in his full dress uniform complete with Samurai sword. She drove in by jeep from the same small local aerodrome that had been attacked some months previously, but stopped the vehicle when spotting the waiting figure, refusing to proceed until he had been removed to the Japanese section out of sight. Only then would she enter the camp. Crowds of jubilant souls besieged her, surrounding the strange looking vehicle, the jeep. Our eminent visitor was neatly dressed in the khaki drill uniform of Commandant of the Red Cross and we were all completely enthralled as she immediately began to distribute copious quantities of boiled sweets and cigarettes. *Real* Players Virginia brand! When the initial excitement had died down, this wonderful lady toured the whole camp, visiting every hut, and afterwards made her way to our 'stage' to address the assembled inhabitants. We were told that she was touring as many camps as possible to bring succour to all she could and to learn at first hand of the terrible conditions that we had endured. It would seem that the tour had met with objections from the military authorities who considered that the venture would be too dangerous, so she just told her husband that she was going and that was that.

One adventuresome man mentioned to her that she was the first white woman, in fact almost the only woman, we had seen for nearly four years. Her response was to advise that soon we would all have some nice nurses to look after us and that she would endeavour to see that they were the most decorous that could be found.

The whole camp, British and other nationalities alike, were

all most impressed and could hardly believe that it was not a dream. I had by now acquired a small notelet book, bought with funds from our first advance of pay, and during the free period when we languished in Nakhon Pathom I jotted down some of my thoughts. Among them was the following verbatim extract:

"Today, here in our ex. POW camp at Nakhon Pathom, Thailand, we were honoured with the visit of Lady Louis Mountbatten. She passed through the camps containing the heavy sick and was sympathy itself. She climbed aboard the wooden platforms which are our communal beds and knelt and spoke to everyone. In the afternoon she gave a touching speech. She is completely unaffected, pleasant and sincere. What a contrast to some officers I know with their middle class affectation and snobbery. All, British, Australians and Dutch were unanimously pleased. They all voted her a WONDERFUL woman."

This was no social butterfly!

The first departure homeward bound had been the handful of Americans, who had left before Lady Louis' visit. As I bid farewell to Harvey Boatman and his friends, wishing him bon voyage quickly and safely back to good old Houston, Texas, I had to admit to a twinge of envy at his early return home. We were quite naturally getting increasingly itchy feet, there was much clamouring for action, and at last information came through that the British would be flown from Bangkok to Rangoon. To be fit enough to fly, however, it was necessary to have a blood count registering a minimum of 75% and haemoglobin tests had to be carried out. A programme of blood transfusions began for those being below the required figure, but I was fortunate enough to scrape through with a reading of 78%.

The arrangements for the Aussies were to be different and they now busied themselves preparing to travel by train back down to Singapore, for onward shipment by sea to the various ports of Australia. So the migration commenced and it was time to say goodbye to many of my friends among them, especially Terry and Bill. The former requested a couple of my family photographs: "To remember you by", he said. Their parting words to me were *"It was bonzer knowing you, Jack, we almost had you naturalized into Aussie."*

When they had left it was the turn of the first British parties to be on the move, Jack Griffin going with the first batch. Soon the departures gathered momentum until only we few in the heavy sick hut remained awaiting the call and whilst we did so Geordie was ensuring that our treatment was continuing without let or hindrance. He was now administering the new magic drug, Mepacrine, for our malaria and it was already turning my sallow complexion into an even more jaundiced appearance. At last, on the 14th September which was almost one month after the Japanese surrender, it was our turn to parade for boarding the buses that would convey us the thirty miles or so to Bangkok Airport. The last of the British to go, we had left behind the unhappy Dutchmen who were marooned there due to serious developments in Java and Sumatra. They were to remain there for another three months until the Dutch government had come to terms with the Indonesian insurgents who had objected to the return of Dutch rule. It must be remembered that the majority of their POWs were resident in the East Indies, many having been born there, and they had no where else to go.

The bus journey took us through the suburbs and then right into the centre of the capital. We were enthralled to see the brick buildings, tar-macadam roads, the traffic and the population going about their daily business; all these things heralded our return to civilization after years in the jungle camps. The experience was difficult to absorb, it all seemed so **unreal**, and we acted as excitedly as school children on an outing. The arrival at Bangkok Airport proved just as dreamlike when we were greeted by bronzed, well turned out Royal Air Force aircrews and ground staff. I think the biggest treat in my life was the cup of tea complete with milk and sugar that awaited us, together with real bread rolls lavishly spread with butter and filled with utterly delicious corned beef. It was all so indescribably good.

Rows of Dakota transport planes were parked on the apron, ready to fly us on the two hour flight to Rangoon the next day. Meantime accommodation for the night was provided in a big hanger, where we found a large group of men who had flown in earlier from Saigon in Indo-china *(now Vietnam)* and among them to my surprise and delight I found Danny Treacher. As a Post Office telephone engineer he had been employed on the railway wiring party and upon its completion had gone on a working party in the Saigon docks. He was even more pleasantly startled to see me, having been told on good authority that I had died two years previously.

During the evening Danny and I wandered across to the perimeter to have a close look at some huge American Skymaster four-engined aircraft. A crewman was sitting on the steps of one and when we passed by he invited us in for an inspection of the interior; we were dazzled by the sheer size and technology of it all. Afterwards we sat on the grass and shared a drink of his American style ice cold beer, this stranger making it clear that he was pleased to have the opportunity of entertaining us.

CHAPTER 16

GOING HOME

On the morning of 15th September the great adventure started as we boarded the aircraft with no thought whatsoever of any danger, even though none of us had flown before. We would not have shown such equanimity if we had known that one of the twenty-five planes that had left Saigon was destined not to arrive at Rangoon and that all aboard would perish. However no such matters worried us as we filed aboard and took our places on the long aluminium benches that ran along the full length of the plane on each side. Everyone was given a blanket, for warmth at high altitude, and solemnly told that noses should be pinched and blown hard during ascent and again upon descending.

Once airborne we peered down and could see the jungle that had been our home for so long, stretching out below as we passed over the area traversed by railway. There was a hushed silence as we all thought of the 12,364 companions we were leaving behind for ever; one life, it was said, for every sleeper that was laid on that accursed project. I got to thinking of Terry telling me about that speech by Magatamo back in Thanbyzuayat in September 1942 and realised that now we knew only too well that he really meant every word - so many thousands had indeed not lived to be released.

After about half an hour's flying I was invited into the cockpit and spent most of the flight there, seeing for the first time how the advanced radar worked on the small screen as it plotted our free progress. Returning to the bench shortly before we began our descent, I pinched my nose vigorously until the 'pop' eliminated the pain in my ears and then suddenly we were down. Upon alighting we were directed to a reception area adjacent to the runway and there, serving refreshments, we found a group of ladies of the Women's Volunteer Service. Dainty cups of tea with saucers and bowls of fruit salad complete with fresh cream were in our unaccustomed hands in a flash, it was almost like being at a small village fete. Now we really were among our own again - freedom is a **MARVELLOUS** experience.

A short journey by truck took us to Rangoon University, whose fine rambling buildings had been converted into a temporary hospital, where we were all placed under medical supervision. A piping hot shower was the first priority, followed by kitting out in jungle green drill uniform and boots, the latter taking an awfully long time to adjust to. They seemed to be so cumbersome and ungainly. That night there was the luxury of sleeping in a set of pyjamas between gleaming white sheets and it was like being in wonderland.

What impressed me more than anything else now that we had been properly released was the aura of efficiency apparent everywhere, which was such a marked contrast to the bumbling uncouthness that had been endured with our former captors. There had been a great many changes since having been cut off from the world three and a half years before and now we found ourselves under the care of RAPWI *(Repatriation of Allied Prisoners of War and Internees)*, an organization that operated like clockwork. Nothing was too much trouble for them, despite their herculean task.

Arrival in Rangoon afforded the facilities to write our first letters home, our only other communication having been the completion of special forms, whilst still at Nakhon Pathom, which were transposed into telegrams to advise of our safe deliverance. It was a great relief to be in touch once more.

Ships began to sail almost daily direct to the United Kingdom and Jack Griffin, who had preceded me by ten days, left soon after my arrival. There was only time for a short get together, when he told me that he had met up with a mutual friend from home serving with the 14th Army troops who had re-occupied Rangoon. It was Bill Owen and we went off to visit him in a nearby kampong where he was billeted in an upstairs basha. This contact with someone from home was most exciting, especially when he produced a recent copy of my local newspaper with its columns of parochial news. After watching Bill play for his unit in an evening football match, Jack and I returned to the university buildings. He was leaving the next morning and promised to call upon Joan on arriving home and assure her that I was alright and would be following him shortly. I also took the opportunity to request him to deliver a long detailed letter personally.

Shortly after Jack had departed we learned that an important person had expressed a wish to address us and instructions were issued for everyone to assemble by the steps leading up to the University main entrance. A small convoy of vehicles drove up and sitting in the front seat of one of the jeeps was an elegant figure dressed in jungle green but wearing a Naval Officer's cap set at a jaunty angle. It was none other than the Supreme Commander of South East Asia, Lord Louis Mountbatten - the King's cousin. As his vehicle came to a halt he jumped out and bounded up the steps, gathering us all around him and beginning an informal chat, expressing his deep honour to greet us in person and to say how much he admired our fortitude in adversity. It was, he felt, the least he could do to bring us up to date and went on to outline the events of the past 'missing' years. After this he jocularly enquired of the whereabouts of his wife, stating that he understood that she had ignored the advice of his commanders and had been up to see us in Thailand. He then commented that she always seemed to have just left whenever he arrived anywhere. Somebody called out to say how kind she had been and reminded him of her promise to ensure we would be looked after by decorative nurses; his reply pointed out that he was arranging for all available passenger shipping to be allocated to get us home as quickly as possible and he would see to it personally that adequate 'troop comforts' would be provided. It was so very relaxed and impressive. Both Lord and Lady Louis, these very important people with the many problems of their high positions to cope with, had gone out of their way to help and comfort us. It was deeply appreciated and earned our enduring respect.

As each day passed the benefit of a balanced diet and close medical attention helped me to become stronger and stronger and, with the prophylactic mepacrene keeping the malaria at bay, after two weeks I was passed fit enough to travel. At the end of September I left hospital for a tented staging camp in readiness for boarding the SS Chitral, a P&O vessel of 23,000 tonnes, but on arrival we ran into an unexpected snag. The ship had been put under quarantine due to a suspected outbreak of bubonic plague on board among the Lascar crew, so there was further delay as we waited for several days before clearance.

Lord Louis' promise to give priority to the allocation of the ships to ex POWs did not make him very popular with the 14th Army lads. It seemed that there was a ruling stipulating that the standard period of service in the Far East had been fixed at three years and four months, so those who had completed this time naturally felt that they were entitled to go home at once. Nevertheless we had no qualms about this as all had been in captivity for longer and some, including myself, had come out six years before and we did not feel too badly about them having to wait awhile. In fact some of the regular soldiers in the Surreys and other units had been away for so long as thirteen years, having been approaching the completion of their normal overseas service when the war broke out in 1939.

I made two more new friends during the wait at the staging camp, forty-six year old Aubrey Tutt from Raynes Park in London, who was a veteran of the Battle of the Marne in the Great War, and Fred Burch of Croydon in Surrey. They had both been in Saigon and the latter was still recovering from beriberi, but by the time we had arrived home he was completely cured.

The plague scare having proved to be a false alarm, we embarked on the 2nd October after first being conveyed across the river by landing craft. On board were 2,222 ex prisoners-of war and 84 former civilian internees, most of whom were accommodated on the mess decks. The senior NCOs were segregated from the other ranks and I shared a cabin with five other sergeants, which was very comfortable indeed. What a contrast to my outward journey and the hammocks on that terrible old coal burning Nevasa! I soon settled down to enjoy the benefits of the bracing sea voyage and the excellent food, even if there was a near good natured riot on the first day out when we were served with *rice pudding*. I suspect that the ship's quartermaster had a fine sense of humour.

Our first port of call was Colombo, where a great fuss was made of us all by the people ashore and I really felt free now that I was on territory that had not been contaminated by Japanese occupation. Renewing my acquaintance of 1940, I toured this delightful city in the company of Aubrey and Fred, taking the opportunity of visiting a studio to be photographed together.

After a one day stay it was full steam ahead again. Before leaving we had to vacate our cabins, the accommodation being taken by a party of fifty Wrens who had now joined the ship for the rest of the voyage. They were there on the express wish of Lord Louis to 'comfort' us and their presence certainly brightened up the atmosphere, being a welcome relief from the continuous male company

From left to right. Myself, Fred and Aubrey.

that we seemed to have been putting up with for ever. My fellow sergeants and I were quite happy to join the other ranks on the less comfortable mess decks; I could also now see more of Fred and Aubrey.

The ship's captain was a spruce white bearded sailor who was quite determined to get us home in record time, planning to arrive at the end of the month. This meant by-passing Bombay and we sailed across the Indian Ocean, then on through the Red Sea to Suez. As we moved in to moor we had the strange experience of watching German prisoners of war working as dockhands and I felt a pang of sympathy for them in their plight. I wondered how long it would be before they too went home like ourselves and could only reflect on my father's comment that "Some day we shall all be together again and that goes for all mothers' sons in all countries."

With the next stop England, it was necessary to delay for two days to enable the issue of winter clothing. Trying on the coarse serge battledress and wearing a tie seemed most strange and cumbersome but we adapted to it in due course. I was however still in some difficulty with heavy army boots.

The greatest joy of all here was the anticipation of receiving our very first mail, but the reality of it for many proved to be disastrous, jolting us out of the euphoria that had been experienced ever since that wonderful day of August 16th. When we paraded for mail distribution I was surprised that neither of the two letters for me were in the handwriting of either of my parents. Blessedly there was one from my dear Joan and the other had come from my elder brother, so I happily opened and read that marvellous first letter from her. Turning to the other one, I found that it contained two letters in my brother's hand and both brought very bad news. One had been dictated by my father and it informed me that my dear mother had passed away in June 1943 *(before any news of my whereabouts had been received)*; he then went on to say that he too had been unwell and was not fit enough to write the letter in his own hand. Brother Bert wrote that father was terminally ill with cancer and that the army had sent him home from India earlier in the year on compassionate leave to be with Dad during his last days. He had also been long away when mother had died, having been posted to Persia in 1942, prior to moving on to India. It was all so very, very sad and I was not alone that unhappy day, many others also suffering bereavements - we had all been away so long. There were as well numerous instances of wives and sweethearts having given people up for dead and marrying either Americans or Canadians.

My parents, Albert and Louise, as they were when we parted in 1939.

Sailing away with heavy hearts, we next made our way up along the Suez Canal to Port Said. Only stopping here for a couple of hours and remaining on board, we were amused to see that the 'bum boatmen' were still active and doing a roaring trade with a French troopship en route for French Indo-China. Now more wordlywise in everyway than we had been six years previously we, though, were no longer prey to these rascals. The Frenchmen were part of the forces being sent out East by the French in an endeavour to restore their rule, which in fact was the beginning of the Vietnam troubles; the Japanese had lost the war decisively but their period of occupation had brought about a strong sense of nationalism throughout the whole of South East Asia.

Moving on through the Mediterranean Sea, we reached Gibraltar, hoving to outside just long enough to pick up more mail. There were shoals of letters for me here, from relatives and friends, no more containing any bad news, thank goodness. The weather was becoming distinctly colder and it was time to change from tropical clothing into the cumbersome battledress. After all those years of constant sunshine the wintry conditions came as something of a shock as we sailed through the choppy sea in the Bay of Biscay, which proved to be most unpleasant and for the first time ever I was violently seasick for two whole days. Once out of the Bay however I shook it off, even though heavy gales persisted until we had entered the English Channel.

I stared with disbelief at the sight of the English coast as we moored outside Southampton on the evening of the 28th of October and rested there for the night. In the morning the town could be seen quite clearly and we gazed with wonder at red brick buildings of the typically English architecture, which contrasted so vividly with the jungle environment from whence we had come. Moving in to berth, we crammed the port side decks to get a first close up look at dear old England and could see that the quayside was decorated with flags and bunting. The band of the King's Royal Rifle Corps were playing at the water's edge and as we halted they struck up the National Anthem, which was followed by cheers from hundreds of officials, dock workers and visitors that included a number of army generals and local dignitaries. To the accompaniment of a selection of popular tunes by the musicians, an official welcoming party came aboard and a message from His Majesty King George V1 was read out over the ship's intercom system by Major-General

Curtis, Commander of the Aldershot and Hampshire District. The King thanked us all for our courage and fortitude in our dark days and expressed his sorrow over the treatment to which we had been subjected.

The great moment finally arrived. As I descended the gangplank I found myself on the same wharf from where we had departed just six years before, China bound via Cherbourg. Transport was waiting to ferry us to our immediate destination which was a reception camp on Southampton Common, where we were to stay overnight. The day was spent firstly with a full medical inspection, all very detailed and thorough; when asked how much of the local tobacco I had smoked, with its inherent dangers, I was thankful to have given up the habit soon after entering Thailand. Next came a concentrated debriefing which entailed the completion of special forms giving details of everyone's experiences, with particular references to atrocities. What we had to tell was collated to be used in evidence in the forthcoming war criminal trials of our former captors, who were now in custody.

Strange looking and unfamiliar ration cards were issued, valid initially for one month, and we also received pay for the same period. There was also a railway warrant to cover the cost of the final part of the journey home and, lastly, we received medal ribbons for the Pacific Star and Defence Medal *(the one for the 1939/45 Medal had already been given to us in Rangoon)*. All formalities over, I was given permission to use the public telephone in the canteen to ring my family that evening, to say that I would be with them the very next day.

I was up and about very early in the morning and stood outside our Nissen hut watching the local people going about their daily routine, with the workers busily cycling to work. Everything was so normal. How was it possible that our own lives had been so rudely turned upside-down over the past six years?

It seemed an eternity before departing, but at last the order came to embus for the railway station to take the train for Waterloo in London. We were soon speeding through the gorgeous Hampshire countryside and I spent the whole time peering out of the window. How GREEN the grass was, how *fat* the cows! What sheer beauty! By mid morning we had pulled into Platform 11 and upon alighting were confronted yet once again with superb efficiency.

Numerous officials had set up tables right there on the plat-

I await, 2nd from left on upper deck, to take my turn for disembarkation from M.V. Chitral at Southampton. 29th October, 1945.

form and when we reported to them they called out our names on the loud speaker system, enabling waiting relatives to find us more easily. Within minutes I was being greeted by a fellow sergeant, my elder brother Bert. It was a joyous reunion and as we chatted away I was surprised by the strangeness of his unaccustomed Middlesex accent.

Immediately we had been reunited a lady from the Red Cross organization approached and asked for my destination. When told she explained that a car was waiting and it would give her much pleasure to drive us both directly home, some twenty miles away. She was one of a team driving a fleet of cars to provide a similar service to all ex POWs living in the Home Counties. Motoring down through the environs of South London and on into South West Middlesex, I was torn between overflowing conversation and bewildering wonderment at the whole scene of streets, buildings and traffic. All this, especially the traffic, was going to take some getting used to.

Before long we were driving along Egham High Street and turning into Limes Road, making all of my dreams come true. As we stopped my five sisters could be seen standing in the doorway of Ferndene, the kind Red Cross lady drove off and I was home, being greeted with a kiss from my poor, emaciated sick father. After six long years my caravan had rested. Goodbye Gypsy.